UNCOVERED

UNCOVERED

WHAT **REALLY** HAPPENS AFTER THE STORM, FLOOD, EARTHQUAKE OR FIRE

MARK GOLDWICH

Published and distributed by:
High-Pitched Hum Publishing
321 15th Street North
Jacksonville Beach, Florida 32250

Contact High-Pitched Hum Publishing at: www.highpitchedhum.net

High-Pitched Hum
Publishing

Dedication

TO INSURANCE CONSUMERS everywhere who know enough to buy insurance, but not enough about the insurance they buy. May this book give them the information they need, the vision to see beyond the hype, and the determination never to be victimized again.

Acknowledgments

MY GRATEFUL THANKS go to my family, especially Zachary, Jordyn, and Tamara. You don't just wake me up every day, you are the reason I keep going, day after day.

Special thanks, too, go to Pegine Echevarria and Brandon Toropov, for convincing me that I had a story, and helping me to tell it.

Table of Contents

I. Consider This

I RECENTLY SPOKE with a client whose home had suffered major damage during a natural disaster. He was uneasy about something, but I couldn't figure out what it was.

We met at a Dunkin Donuts near his home. He took his seat at the little circular table and carefully removed the plastic lid of his coffee cup. His lips were pursed and he wouldn't meet my gaze.

He told me that he wanted me to stop working on his claim against his insurance company. I was a little taken aback by this, because things had been going quite well on the claim. So I asked him why he would want me to stop work.

"You've already gotten me over $38,000 more than they said they were going to pay me," he said. "You're doing a great job, but I just don't know if I can afford to pay you." He had forgotten that I wasn't charging him an out-of-pocket fee, but instead a small percentage of what I recovered for him *above* what the insurance company had offered to pay.

Frankly, I think he was ...

... used to being taken advantage of.

After all, that's what he felt had happened with his insurance company, and he expected the trend to continue in his relationship with me.

I explained to him that if I got him another, say, $25,000, he would get $22,500, and I would get $2,500 – *after* the check from the insurance company came in. **Translation: No money was coming out of his pocket. Ever.**

"Hmm..."

He thought for a moment, smiled, and told me to go for it. Good thing, too, because within a week, I had tracked down another $27,775 in valid claims for him, followed by another $9,300 or so before the claim was settled. In all, his settlement went from $12,029 to over $87,583. All with no out-of-pocket expenses for him whatsoever.

He now understands how a public adjuster works. But my experience is that he's in the minority. Most people who suffer through natural disasters *don't* realize that a good public adjuster is someone they want on their side. Most people get so numbed, or enraged, or both, by the experience of dealing with an insurance company that they come to assume that everyone is out to get them.

It's an understandable reaction.

II. What People Overlook

HERE'S WHAT PEOPLE typically overlook: Insurance companies are businesses. You may say, "I know that." And I'm sure you do. But do you know what it really *means* – how that fact is actually going to affect *your* life when you file a claim?

If you've ever tried to collect on a claim after a major disaster such as a fire, flood, or hurricane, you probably *do* know what it really means when I say that the insurance company is a business, first and foremost. On the other hand, *if* you have not yet had this experience, or are just beginning it, then this book should definitely be considered "required reading" for you, because you probably *don't* yet know what I'm really saying when I tell you that insurance companies are businesses, first and foremost.

For instance:

You may think, because you pay insurance companies to protect you against risks, that you are the "customer" or "client" of the insurance company.

While this may be technically true, thinking in that way can be a big mistake.

If you think of yourself as the "customer" or "client," you will expect certain principles of "customer service" to guide the relationship after an unexpected event affects your property. You will also expect the insurance company to be accountable to you in a way that's roughly similar, say, to the way a furniture store is responsible for delivering furniture in a timely fashion once someone has selected, and paid for, the goods.

You will almost certainly be disappointed.

As someone with 20 years of experience as an insurance adjuster, working on both the insurance company side and the insurance consumer side, I'm here to tell you a hard truth.

You may *want* to be treated as a "customer", and you may *want* the insurance company to be accountable – to fulfill its obligations to you without you having to do much beyond routine paperwork. **Alas, it doesn't necessarily work out like that.**

Often, you are simply regarded as the next in a very long line of people who are trying to take more from the insurance company than you deserve. The working assumption is likely to be that your claim is not justified, even when it is.

Rather than using the "customer/client" metaphor you are entitled to use, I want to suggest that you may be better served by using another metaphor to guide your decisions when you find yourself in need of payment on an insurance claim.

The metaphor I suggest you use is the one where you think of the insurance company as your *legal adversary.*

Why do I say that? It's really not because I represent people who have claims against insurance companies. It's because that is how insurance companies tend to treat the people they cover: as one would treat a legal adversary.

III. Diamonds And Rocks

CONSIDER YOURSELF THE LEGAL ADVERSARY of your insurance company. If you feel uneasy about this advice, you should carefully consider the following **true story.**

When I was a young adjuster working for a big insurance company, part of our job was meeting with local agents to maintain good relationships. Now, you would think that working for the same company would be a strong bond between these two groups of people, but keep in mind, agents and adjusters have totally different perspectives.

At the time, agents were independent contractors who worked for, and were paid based on, commissions that came from the policyholders. The adjuster, on the other hand, worked for the insurance company, and is often at odds with the policyholders (as I have suggested here).

Back in the 'old days,' agents would call the claims department and say, "This guy is taking us for a ride, don't pay him anything!" Or perhaps the agent would call the claims department and say, "I've known these folks for years, we go to the same church, and they would never ask for anything if it wasn't owed to them. Do me a favor, stop messing around and pay this claim!" In some cases, it was a matter of "never mind the facts, just do what I say." Agents carried a lot of weight back then.

I will never forget one meeting I had with an agent who was known to be a bit crusty, especially when claims weren't handled to his liking. This agent was trying to explain to me why he had complaints about claim handling.

He drew a box and said, "Here is the insurance store. I am in the front selling *diamonds,* and when the customer goes around back to pick up his diamonds, you guys in claims are back there handing out *rocks!"*

In other words, he was selling peace of mind and security from a top-rated national company with the promise of world-class customer service whenever a claim needed to be filed. And we (the people in claims) were simply not delivering the product he was selling. That's what he was telling me.

Because I was young, because I was idealistic, because I was a good "company man," I was genuinely insulted by this implication. In fact, I thought this agent was just a world-class jerk.

After two decades of dealing with the insurance industry, however, I am here to inform you that he was absolutely right.

Now, you might well ask: *Who won the battle between the agents and the claims department?* Guess.

Most agents for this particular company are now more like employees than independent contractors. They do what they're told. And there's even a written guideline at this company that specifically states that agents are not to interfere with the way claims are handled. In case you're keeping score, that's two points for Claims, and zero points for Agents (as well as the policyholders they are *supposed* to represent). That crusty old agent knew exactly what was happening in the industry, and he didn't like it one bit. I figured it out eventually. Now you have the opportunity to learn, too, perhaps before you get burned.

> # Consider the insurance company your adversary.

If you're at all skeptical about this admonition, know that I wrote this book with you in mind. And keep reading.

IV. Two Disasters

THE FIRE, FLOOD, HURRICANE OR TORNADO that descends on a community is one kind of disaster, and it's easy for the victim to recognize as such. Even an isolated event, like a pipe leak or a theft, can be disastrous to a business or homeowner. The difference is, those kinds of disasters are *easy to recognize as such,* and most people realize that they must be prepared for them.

What happens to the people who then try to secure the insurance compensation they're entitled to is, all too often, another kind of disaster. And it's *that second* disaster, I submit, that you are not expecting, and are probably unprepared for. Literally millions of people have been victimized by the second kind of disaster after having endured the first kind. The saddest thing about it is this: most victims of the second type of disaster *do not even realize that the second disaster has taken place.*

Think about it. If you don't know what is covered and why it's covered ... or how to identify and estimate all the damages you've sustained ... or how to determine what you should actually get paid ...

...how would you know whether the insurance company was holding back when it came to compensating you fully for valid claims?

How would you know?

Even if you were to figure out the insurance company was, through error, oversight, or any other reason, not paying you all it should ... you would still have to convince the insurance company that you were right and they were wrong. That is not something they are particularly fond of admitting.

If you believe, as I do, that one disaster at a time is quite enough, you'll want to consider the contents of this book very carefully indeed.

V. Three Things Insurance Companies Don't Want You To Know

THERE ARE THREE THINGS insurance companies would rather you didn't know are very likely to happen after the disaster.

Ask someone who's been through this.

- *The first thing insurance companies don't want you to know:* No matter how well you hold up your end of the bargain, there may be extensive **DELAYS** throughout the entire claim process.

You will find that your calls don't go through, or you will leave a message (either via voicemail or through a message service), that never seems to get returned.

This can go on for weeks or months.

Eventually, you may be informed that some other

company is "handling" the job of sending an adjuster out to look at your loss ... and you may figure out that that company, in turn, has passed the job on to yet another company. This "hand-off" phase may continue until two, three or four layers of bureaucracy are built up. Then you will learn that an appointment has to be made, an estimate has to be written, a payment has to be approved –- and you will see that each step brings additional, unexpected, and incomprehensible delays.

All the while, everybody you talk to will assure you that the delay and unresponsiveness is somebody else's fault. But no one will take action to speed up the process.

Time is on the side of the insurance companies, and they know it. The idea seems to be that if they can put you off long enough, you will quit, forget about the whole business, take whatever they offer, or (quite literally) *die* before they have to pay up.

- *The second thing insurance companies don't want you to know.* They will often **DENY COVERAGE** for all or part of the loss. Either intentionally or unintentionally, the insurance company will report – often wrongly – that your loss is not covered.

If you're covered for wind damage, they may say the damage was caused by water.

If you're covered for water damage, they may say it was caused by winds.
If you're covered for both, they may say it was caused by

a combination that they can't cover, or they may say the damage was actually caused by something else. In my experience, the rule is a reliable one: You will be told by someone, at some point in time, in some way or another, that your policy covers less than you thought it covers.

- *The third thing insurance companies don't want you to know:* They can **DEFLECT RESPONSIBILITY** for actually paying you.

Your loss may, in theory, be covered ... but you may learn (perhaps long after the fact) that you didn't document the claim precisely as required, or that the adjuster was unable to tell exactly what caused the damage, or that some other problem held up processing. Typically, you may learn that someone who seems to be an employee of the insurance company actually represents an entirely different organization.

When you try to figure out who's actually responsible for delivering on obligations to you, you may not be able to track anyone down.

Again, time is on the side of the insurance industry. For a shockingly large percentage of these situations, the deflection of responsibility results in people with valid claims simply walking away from the situation.

You may find out about these problems when it's too late to do anything. You'll listen helplessly as somebody from the insurance company explains how they wish they could pay you, but they can't because of the lapse in time (a window that nobody told you about), because of the company's policy, because of some obscure regulation, because of a recalcitrant boss, or because of some equally creative explanation. It's not their fault; they can't do anything about it.

Ask someone who's been through this.

VI. The 30/180/365 Principle

IT SHOULD, in theory, take about thirty days to process a valid insurance claim after a major disaster. And that's what most policyholders imagine will be required to sort things out. A month. Perhaps two.

In practice, though, my experience is that it can take between 180 days and *one full year* to process that claim.

Believe it or not, the 180-to-365-day window is what you can expect if the system is operating on a *normal* case, without significant complications.

That's what happens if things go *smoothly*. If there are major problems or disputes as to the coverage, scope of damages, method of repair, or payment amount, the process can drag on for much, much longer!

Ask someone who's been through this.

This is real. This is not something I'm making up. This changes peoples' lives, and not for the better. It's hard to express the level of frustration people feel when a claim is delayed, especially for such (seemingly) inexplicable lengths of time. People have other things going on in their lives. They often have medical problems. They could be moving. They have work issues. They may have family members who are in need of extra assistance. Whatever they're facing, policyholders often reach a point where they just want to move on to the next chapter in their lives.

They get frustrated. They feel out of their element and overwhelmed by all the paperwork, all the questions, and all the details. They just do not want to deal with insurance companies anymore. They tell themselves that they really do not care how much they lose -- they just want to "wrap it all up."

By an extraordinary coincidence, that mentality, and the delays that produce it, combine to keep the insurance companies from having to pay out a great deal of money.

People simply do not realize how much they are losing by voluntarily entering that "just wrap it up" phase of their insurance claim. All they know for certain is that they cannot stand the delay for another day. They want it over with. *Consider these questions.*

- Does the insurance company benefit from someone getting so fed up with the claims process that he or she "settles" for a certain amount, so as to finally "be done with it"?

- Does that process of wanting to "be done with it" and walking away from the claims process, happen once or twice or three times after a natural disaster ... or does it happen hundreds, thousands, or even *hundreds of thousands* of times? (In 2004, there were over 2.4 million hurricane claims in the state of Florida alone!)

- If *you* were one of the people considering walking away from the claims process six months, or eight months, or a full year after initiating the claims process, would you be at all interested to learn what your decision to walk away would be likely to cost you?

Not uncommon: fifty thousand dollars.

If you knew you were losing, say, *fifty thousand dollars* because the insurance company has dragged its heels for months ... would you still say that you "couldn't bear the delay any longer" or "couldn't handle the hassle anymore"?

Or would you agree that it made sense to have someone on your side, an expert, continue to look into the claim on your behalf?

I've never heard of a representative for an insurance company coming out and admitting to the media (or anyone else) that the company delays paying claims so that people will give up and walk away from the process.

I've never heard an insurance company official say that

they actually *try* to bump up a thirty-day job so that it lasts six months, or eight months, or twelve months, in order to drive people away out of sheer frustration.

And I've never had an insurance company admit that it was routinely dragging out the process so that it wouldn't have to pay policyholders millions of dollars in valid claims.

Those things only happen in the movies.

All I can tell you about is the coincidences. Delays do happen. And those delays benefit the insurance companies financially – and hurt the policyholders who walk away. That's the coincidence we have to deal with. That's reality.

Believe it: The delays go on for so long that, in my experience, some policyholders actually *die* before they settle. This is an outcome that also benefits the insurance company, inasmuch as dead people tend to dispute fewer claims than living ones. Chalk it up to coincidence. Again.

You may well ask: Why do the coincidences always seem to benefit the multi-million or multi-billion dollar company -- and never seem to benefit the individual policyholder?

It could be because insurance companies *are* so big and powerful. It could be because most people are not trained to recognize and deal with the waves of post-disaster coincidences that always seem to benefit the insurance industry. It could even be the insurance industry plays more than a bystander's role when it comes to influencing the environments in which these coincidences occur.

Ask someone who's been through this.

VII. Three Reasons People Choose To Get A Public Adjuster On Their Side

THE "BIG THREE" reasons are as follows.

- *Reason number one:* The delays drive people so crazy that they want to walk away from the process, and I help them do that responsibly. Public adjusters, like me, take over the handling of the claim for them. I relieve them of the aggravation and stress that cripples so many (insurance) disaster victims. I represent them and their interests to the insurance company *responsibly* -- so they can get on with their lives, keep their sanity, and get the compensation for their loss that they deserve.

- *Reason number two:* Public adjusters only charge based on what they actually recover. There is no up-front or out-of-pocket expense to hire me. Ever. That's the way a public adjuster works. (If a public adjuster asks you for a retainer or for up-front money, run in the opposite direction as fast as you can!)

- *Reason number three:* Qualified public adjusters are property insurance experts. People realize that, if the playing field is to be leveled, they need an expert on their side to counter the significant resources of the insurance company. Because of my expertise, I get results for policyholders: consistent, dramatic, measurable results.

As an example of what I mean, let me just tell you that I've taken a claim that was, according to the insurance company, supposedly worth just $7,000 in payments to the policyholder – a claim that the emotionally exhausted policyholder was ready to walk away from – and secured *$140,000* in payments on *valid* claims for my client.

In that case, walking away would have cost the policyholder over $130,000! How happy do you suppose this individual was that a neighbor recommended me?

The moral of the story is:

Don't walk away from a claim.

Get me (or someone like me) to handle the runaround -- effectively. Once you do, you won't have to worry about the specifics that turn what should be a 30-day claim into a 180-day or a 365-day nightmare. Dealing with those specifics is my job. It shouldn't have to be yours.

So you can understand why it's so important to *have* someone like me to handle the runaround and, shorten it for you ... let me preview for you the specific delaying maneuvers – or, if you prefer, the coincidences – that will almost certainly stack up against you when you file a claim with your insurance company after a natural disaster or other insured loss.

Read on. If you dare.

VIII. Early-Phase Delays

IN THIS CHAPTER, I want to show you examples of what I call *early-phase* delays. These are delays that come in the first stage, the stage immediately following the disaster or insured loss.

These examples of delay are sometimes the most shocking ones to people who file claims, because they expect to be treated as customers, rather than adversaries, by their insurance company. (By the time policyholders get to mid-phase and late-phase delays, they're not quite as shocked by the behavior of some insurance companies and other players who are supposed to represent their interests.)

Q&A: What will happen

• **Will there be enough manpower to process the claims that (predictably) follow a natural disaster?** No. A cynic might tell you that this manpower shortage is intentional. I can't *know* what the intentions of large organizations like insurance companies are, so all I will be able to say for sure is that, the insurance company will not have enough people on the ground to process the deluge of claims that will follow a major fire, flood, hurricane, tornado, or other significant event. By a remarkable coincidence, this works to their financial benefit.

And believe it or not, this "manpower shortage coincidence" takes place over and over again, year after year.

• **You mean the first few days following the disaster, right? The period before the insurance company "calls in the troops"?** No, I mean a period of weeks or months immediately following the catastrophe that triggers your insurance claim. And for many insurance companies, there really are no full-time "troops" for them to call in.

• **Why not?** Insurance companies generally staff on a permanent basis at a level that's meant to handle claims that take place for more common events like kitchen fires, pipe leaks, thefts, and other routine forms of property damage or loss. In other words, they simply don't *hire* enough permanent claims staff to cover disasters in addition to the more ordinary claims.

• **Is that because insurance companies don't know whether disasters will actually take place in a given twelve-month period?** Given the industry's historic obsession with probability, and with actuarial statistics connected specifically to things like fires, floods, hurricanes, and tornadoes, this seems like an unlikely explanation. Some of the larger insurance companies do hire additional staff to handle catastrophe situations, but certainly not as many as are actually needed.

• Could they *hire* enough full-time staff to do the job for disasters that they know, or strongly suspect, will eventually take place? If you mean "can they afford to," that's a matter best discussed with the executive management teams, boards of directors, and stockholders of insurance companies. Although I'm a former insurance company employee myself, I was not privy to these sorts of internal decisions in any meaningful detail.

• Yeah, but on April 5, 2006, didn't the Los Angeles Times report that "the companies that provide Americans with their homeowners and auto insurance made a record $44.8-billion profit last year" -- meaning 2005 – the year of Hurricane Katrina and the other big storms? Yes, the *LA Times* did in fact report that. By the way, on April 18, 2007, the Insurance Information Institute reported that 2006 profits increased to a mind-boggling *$63.7 billion* dollars!

• So how *do* they process the claims if they don't have the manpower on staff to handle them? Basically, they outsource. In much the same way that Information Technology companies outsource programming and technical service jobs to other countries, insurance companies utilize independent adjusting firms that subcontract with adjusters who can be sent to a disaster site to work for an insurance company.

• What happens when there *isn't* a disaster? If there is nothing going on in the form of insurance work, then these people have to fend for themselves. Some are able to work year-round for insurance companies. Many others go back to whatever work they did before deciding to be Independent Adjusters. And still others just wait for the next disaster, living for extended periods off money made working the last disaster – semi-retired, I call them. (Some companies even "outsource" to departments within their own company. It sounds like a contradiction in terms, but I do know of at least one company that has a separate claims department within the company that handles and charges for catastrophe claims on a per file basis. One part of the company pays another part of the company to handle a portion of the company's claims.)

• **What kinds of credentials are adjusters required to have?** Less than you might think. In many states, they don't have to have a college degree or even need to be licensed. Even in states which require a license, the Independent Adjusters don't need to be licensed *before* the storm; they simply get "temporary" or "emergency" licenses once they start working for the insurance company. They could literally be hauling manure one day, and adjusting your loss the next.

• **Yes, but once a storm hits, there are lots of them swinging quickly into action, right?** The insurance companies would say yes, and you can be sure there will be a news clip with at least *one* adjuster quickly on the scene looking appropriately concerned. Even so, my personal experience is that there are not nearly enough adjusters getting to the site when they should, and I believe most storm victims would agree with me. Ultimately, the answer depends on one's definitions of the words "lots", "quickly", and "action." I can predict, confidently, that *you* won't consider the adjuster's appearance to be timely.

• **What's the holdup?** When a storm or other disaster hits, the independent adjusting firms get a call from the insurance company. Their people start calling people, who start calling other people, who start calling still other people. Then the independent adjusting firms start looking for a place to set up their offices, or perhaps they wait for the insurance company to set up facilities. As a practical matter, independent adjusters (who are the people typically given assignments through these companies) are usually left to their own devices when it comes to traveling to the disaster site, finding a hotel to stay at and securing other support services. You can imagine how difficult it is to secure undamaged, available housing and office space right after a disaster. Needless to say this, too, slows down the processing of your claim.

• **What actually happens when I call the insurance company?** *If* you can get through at all, you'll probably get the number of a claims call center.

• **Okay, what happens when I reach the call center?** Typically, they take your information. They can't do much of anything else. Unlicensed call center personnel often can't even tell you how much the deductible is on your policy. These people are temporary employees who are not well trained and (usually) not particularly motivated. They take down the information, either handwritten on a simple store-bought pad or company created sheet of paper, or they may transmit an e-mail or generate a message printout. Each of these calls represents a message that an adjuster working for that company is *supposed* to return. That is, *if* the message gets to the right place. Note that the person who's "supposed" to return your call is *not* an employee of the insurance company. Keep in mind, too, that there may be hundreds or thousands of messages competing with yours for attention in the days following a catastrophe. Very often, these messages are stacking up before there are people in place to do anything with them. Things get lost. Coincidentally, this benefits the insurance company.

- **Let's say I reach the call center. I am now "someone" for this adjuster -- who's probably an independent adjuster -- to get back to. How long is it going to be before I hear from that adjuster to set up a time for inspection of my property?** This is the sixty-four-thousand dollar question. The best answer is that you should probably be prepared to wait anywhere from one week to three months to get even an initial call back. I would suggest if you haven't heard back after a day or two, you should call back – the adjuster probably lost your message. Call, leave message, wait, repeat. Call, plead, leave message, wait, repeat. Call, plead, plead some more, leave message, wait, repeat. Does this really sound like something you'd like to do while you're without power, without air conditioning, without hot meals, and without clean water … for, say, two months?

- **You're kidding, right?** I wish I were. I recently talked to an adjuster on behalf of one of my clients after a natural disaster. When I finally was able to speak to him after weeks and weeks of calling with no response, I asked him to explain his failure to return my messages. He said, "Look, I get 80 messages a day and I have time to return maybe ten of those messages before I get another 80 the next day. That's the system. You do the math."
- **That's an exceptional case, right?** No, I'm afraid that was quite typical for this insurance company – and probably not too different from most other companies. It really is all about

staffing. The call center folks are there, but they can't help. You need to talk to the adjuster. But the adjuster is not there. He or she is out "in the field" adjusting losses. If they were available to talk to you, who would adjust all the losses? Is it a Catch-22, or is it just a coincidence that happens to benefit the insurance company? Whatever it is, it's not going to work out in your favor.

• **Couldn't insurance companies afford to do this differently, given that they're pulling in record profits these days?** One would certainly think so. The question then is at what cost? Odds are the insurance companies would find it too expensive to provide the level of service expected by consumers.

• **So – you're saying that I have to wait a couple of weeks for the insurance company and the independent adjusting company to set things up ... and then another week to three months *more* just to hear back from the adjuster for the first time?** That's pretty much par for the course. Sure, you might get lucky and be the first person the adjuster calls back. You might also win the lottery tonight. I wouldn't count on either.

• **Yeah, but things get better after I hear back from the adjuster, right?** Wrong. I'll tell you all about mid-phase delays in the next chapter.

$$\boxed{\textbf{Read on.}}$$

IX: Mid-Phase Delays

ONCE YOU ACTUALLY hear back from the adjuster, you might imagine that the process would finally start to speed up. Unfortunately, you'd probably be wrong.

"What is holding this *up?*"

It's during this middle phase that people usually conclude that *something* other than the immediate aftermath of the disaster is holding up the processing of their claim. That "something" could well be the greed of insurance companies. Then again, it could be some systemic problem having to do with the institutional nature of any insurance-related bureaucracy.

Maybe greed is not the best explanation for the strange "holding pattern" affecting mainly independent adjusters and insurance companies. This pattern that seems to kick in around about the time the *other* institutions in the affected community – the post office, the hospital, the businesses that weren't physically damaged -- have all started to bounce back from tragedy. But a debilitating malaise seems, predictably, to grip the insurance sector at exactly this point.

It's certainly possible that greed has nothing to do with this malaise. Mid-phase delays in processing your claim *might* not have anything to do with insurance company greed.

Then again, they just might.

Q&A: What will happen

• **Once I get some kind of contact from the adjuster, how high a priority is my specific claim likely to be for this person?** It's likely to be extremely low.

• **Why?** Because catastrophe adjusters tend to have unconscionably high workloads.

• **How heavy a workload are we talking about, exactly?** The adjuster may well be given fifty, one hundred, or two hundred claims. In considering those numbers, bear in mind that he or she could probably only assess between three and five in any given day for a typical disaster.

• **Is that because insurance companies can't afford to hire enough adjusters?** Given the record earnings reported by the industry (see Chapter VIII), this really does not seem to be a plausible explanation.

• **What other explanation could there possibly be for the industry's decision to pile so much work on a single adjuster?** It may have something to do with extraterrestrial intelligence sabotaging a critical Earthling recovery pattern so as to lay the groundwork for a future assault on our planet. On the other hand, if the insurance industry *isn't* under the covert control of off-world civilizations far more advanced than ours, the impossibly high workload of adjusters may have something to do with corporate greed. By a singular coincidence, a fleet of surrealistically overloaded adjusters tends to reduce the speed at which valid claims are evaluated and processed.

• **What has to happen before the adjuster can actually come out and inspect my property?** Typically, the adjuster only has to make some kind of voice-to-voice contact with you over the phone.

• **That can't take all *that* long, can it?** If you're one of the very first people on the list, and you happen to be sitting by the phone waiting for it to ring, no, it won't take long at all. But remember: the adjuster may have fifty, one hundred, or two hundred claims to contact; he or she must sort those claims into some kind of geographic order. The overloaded adjuster can't be expected to drive all around, based on the order the claims were filed – he or she is much more likely to make calls within a small territory before moving on to contact the next area over. Remember this:

Adjusters usually prioritize by severity.

In other words, they try to see the most severely damaged – usually uninhabitable – homes first. This appears to be the most compassionate thing to do, but – by another extraordinary coincidence – it is also the most frugal from the insurance company's point of view. You see, these uninhabitable homes usually require the insurance company to pay "loss of use" expenses. These can be extremely high. But if you get to these claims right away, you can "lock in" timeframes and dollar amounts owed to the policyholder, greatly reducing the overall costs. In some settings, though, the adjuster may be required to call on each policymaker's file before any of them are inspected (that alone could take quite a while). Either way, it starts with a phone call from the adjuster to you. And if you're *not* sitting by the phone when the call comes, you can then expect to wait. You may wait while you and the adjuster play phone tag. You may wait while the adjuster's schedule takes him or her out of your area. You may wait because your file is reassigned to someone else. You may wait because the adjuster gets sick, gets injured, has legal troubles, or simply quits. Whatever happens, though, the odds are that ....

You WILL wait.

• **Suppose I'm unlucky enough to land at or near the bottom of the adjuster's territory/priority list – what does that really mean to me?** It means that you may well have to wait for *every* person, in *every* other territory identified by the adjuster, to talk with the adjuster by phone, schedule a visit, and actually have their property inspected. In other words, your own perceived "place in line," which you probably assume will be based on the point in time that you filed your claim, could end up being pretty much meaningless, since you are now waiting for the adjuster to meet with people who filed claims *much later* than you did. They get to meet the adjuster before you do simply because they're closer to the area where the adjuster is already working.

- **Are there any other ways people could "jump ahead of me" in line?** Yes. They could move up higher on the adjuster's priority list if they get their insurance agent to report the damage as being more severe than it really is. Mind you, the insurance agents would probably never *admit* to engaging in such a callous and self-serving practice, but, back when I was working as an adjuster for a major insurance company, I got the distinct impression this took place. In fact, it seemed to happen so frequently that I couldn't begin to estimate the total number of times I made my way to a supposedly devastated property, only to learn that it had sustained considerably less damage than I had been led to believe.

The bitter truth ...

... is that the system is probably going to make you wait for a period that is much longer than any rational person would consider acceptable. After a major disaster, that's simply what happens, given the manpower, workload, and logistical hurdles that independent adjusters are forced to deal with. So let's face it: It's going to take a while to get to everyone. Some people will jump ahead, and some will fall to the rear, but the overwhelming majority of policyholders are going to be waiting for a whole lot longer than they'd like.

• **Okay. But once the adjuster actually arrives in a given area, things do start to move forward briskly *in that geographical area*, don't they?** Sometimes. Other times, things go mysteriously wrong in ways that cause substantial delays. The insurance companies – buffered as they are by the companies they are outsourcing an ever-increasing amount of their work to – benefit financially from delays that they (technically) have nothing to do with. Call it another in a long list of extraordinary coincidences that benefit their bottom line.

• **It all sounds very fishy – but are there events that can "legitimately" delay an adjuster?** Sure. As we've seen, a claim can be reassigned. It's also quite possible that the adjuster will have to deal with an honest-to-goodness family emergency; we all have those from time to time. Very often, this emergency is disaster-related; some of these people are picked because they're local, and local people have local ties of their own to think of after a hurricane, tornado, earthquake, fire, or flood. Other adjusters come from out of state, which means that they may need to go home when things go wrong there. And, as we've already noted, the adjuster could get into an accident, get sick, get reassigned to another region, or "burn out" and quit the profession – not an uncommon outcome.

• **When an adjuster is reassigned, what happens to all the claims that adjuster was responsible for, but now leaves behind?** All the files have to go to someone entirely new, and

The whole process starts again.

- **Is that a big deal?** Absolutely. Let's say you've been called by Adjuster A, and Adjuster A has set up an inspection time for two weeks from today. The appointment comes and goes. No one shows up. You call the insurance company, get transferred to the call center, spend a whole lot of time on hold, and then, if you're lucky, get the news that that adjuster is no longer handling that file. At that point, you may be given the name and phone number of Adjuster B ... or you may simply be told that you will need to wait for the new adjuster to contact you.

- **Okay, but that's only likely to happen to me once, right?** In my experience, it's not unheard-of for a claim to be reassigned in this way two, three, or more times in succession. Some people end up with a *dozen* or more adjusters by the time the claim is paid.

- **Once the adjuster actually inspects my property, what happens then?** After the adjuster inspects the claim, he or she must write up an estimate, a process that sometimes takes quite a while to complete.

- **Why?** First, understand that you are likely to be dealing with an (outsourced) independent adjuster. The independent adjusters are, typically, hoping to physically inspect a whole bunch of claims *first* ... and then, having done that inspection work write up all the estimates *later*. Why? Because they are afraid that if they don't get out and at least inspect the claims, the claims will be taken away from them and given to somebody else, which means they will lose out on billing for that claim. The independent adjusting industry can be a bit cutthroat. After all, qualifications are minimal, prior experience is not required, and the financial potential is tremendous.

Some are paid $1,000 per day just to make themselves "available" (i.e., sit and wait) from the time the storm strikes to the day they begin working on the storm claims. Some independents can make over $200,000 per year. Just about everybody would *like* to be at that level. Out of fear of losing money, and access to future claims, they want to keep as many claims as possible. So they may put off writing up your estimate so they can go out and inspect more claims.

This is unfortunate for two reasons: first, it delays your payment (there's a surprise), and second, the quality of the estimate drops with the passage of time, because the estimator's memory of your property fades. Even with inspection notes and photos, the passage of time means that there is a greater likelihood of ambiguity, error, and a resulting challenge from the insurance company. (Still more coincidences.)

• **Who is ultimately accountable for customer complaints during this process?** Excellent question. If such a person exists, you have my heartiest wishes for good luck in locating him or her. As a practical matter, all you can do is call the message center. When you do, the person who answers the phone will tell you repeatedly that he or she can do nothing more than take a message for you.

As I pointed out earlier: There are really *two* disasters to deal with: one that everybody knows about because they see it on the news, and one that you only know about if you yourself actually experience it. **That second disaster has to do with actually getting money from your insurance policy.**

• **Do policyholders ever go crazy as a result of dealing with this stuff?** Not being a qualified mental health professional, I am in no position to say. But the question has certainly crossed my mind. Imagine the level of frustration that somebody will feel after having suffered damage from a hurricane, fire, flood or other calamity – then waiting for weeks to hear from an adjuster -- and then having new adjuster after new adjuster delay, then leave a voice mail, then set up a time to meet, and fail to materialize. I wouldn't be surprised to learn that some people do in fact need counseling and/or therapy as a result of dealing with the claims process. I do know that, as a public adjuster, I deal with these kinds of problems constantly, and they are *extremely* frustrating -- even for me. And I'm already *familiar* with this process of ongoing, systemic delay. Dealing with it is what I choose to do for a living!

• **Is that all I have to worry about when it comes to delays?** I wish it were. Read on. I'll tell you all about late-phase delays in Chapter X.

X: Late-Phase Delays

THERE IS YET another phase of the "delay problem." This phase takes place after the insurance company's estimator has completed the initial estimate.

The good news is that, unless your claim is denied (a prospect we'll cover in another part of the book) you are probably going to be talking about specifics that are actually related to your claim from this point forward. There's a relief!

The bad news is that you're probably *going* to be talking about the specifics for much longer than you had in mind. And you may not like what you hear.

Q&A: What will happen

• **Once there's an actual estimate, what's likely to slow the process down?** It's possible (and, indeed, likely) that essential things have been left out of the estimate the adjuster comes up with. Sometimes the estimate is so low that, if you accepted it, you would not even be able to afford to *start* the work necessary to complete repairs. This may be the result of an honest oversight on the part of an overworked estimator; it may be because the estimator is not quite diligent enough when it comes to identifying valid claims. In either case, you may well end up looking at an estimate that is inadequate to your needs. And that will definitely slow you down.

In all likelihood, the insurance adjuster will say that there is a logical explanation for the difference between what you expected to get and what the insurance company is offering. The adjuster may say, for instance, that the shortfall is there because the cost of the repair work is within your deductible, or because the adjuster took depreciation into account on items that call for replacement cost, or because the insurance company has decided not to pay your contractor's overhead until it is incurred, or even because they believe a contractor would be charging too much to do the work. All of those sound like good excuses. And they all may be distractions from the real problem. Personally, I'd be looking closely at the estimate for items that the adjuster "accidentally" left off.

- **What happens if I can't get the adjuster to raise the amount?** You have two options. *Option one:* You can walk away from the process and take what the insurance company gives you, or you can continue to pursue the claim and demand a re-inspection. (*Important note:* If you simply authorize the work you think is needed done and then submit your bills to the insurance company, the odds are very good that the insurance company will consider your action to be tantamount to walking away from the process, which means that you are very unlikely to get your repairs paid for.) *Option two:* You can continue to pursue the claim.

Hiring an attorney, or a public adjuster like me, would fall under continuing to pursue the claim. Unless you are positive the insurance company made a mistake and *overpaid* the claim in error, I always strongly recommend pursuing the claim aggressively. You might, for instance, work with someone like me, who might advise you to demand a re-inspection.

• **If I demand a re-inspection, doesn't that mean the whole process starts all over again?** Not quite, but it can certainly create additional delays. However, at this stage of the game, your choice is pretty simple: Accept what they are offering to pay you -- or accept additional delays in order to pursue the additional monies you are entitled to.

• **What if no re-inspection is needed – won't the adjuster just write me a check?** Not unless the amount of additional money you are asking for is very small. (And if the insurance company does that, the odds are not good that you'll be getting a check big enough to actually repair the damage you have suffered.)

Consider: Many insurance companies now have entire teams set up to handle "supplemental" claims. These are claims that are made because the initial payment was disputed as being too low. There's a *reason* so many adjusters are working on supplemental teams. *Insurance companies dispute a lot of stuff.* The adjusters on these teams are trained to resolve these claims over the phone if possible. Would it surprise you to learn that a phone-handled claim costs less than a field-handled claim?

• **What *will* the adjuster do?** The adjuster will give the claim file material to a supervisor or file examiner, and the file examiner will then have to review the claim. Of course, it could be weeks before the file examiner even *sees* your claim.

The examiner will either approve it or kick it back down to the field adjuster (probably not the original adjuster, of course.) Which of these two is more likely? It's hard to say, because every case is different. But keep in mind that these offices are flagrantly understaffed. Some of the people who work there are often shockingly inexperienced. I personally know of cases where the claim examiner had literally *never* inspected a claim before. And yet this is the person who is directing, and rejecting, estimates written by *seasoned* adjusters! By the way, the examiner might be handling the estimates for five adjusters, or might be responsible for as many as twenty. You have no way of knowing.

One thing's for certain: The claim examiner inevitably has a huge stack of estimates to review, a stack that gets bigger and bigger with each passing day. So that's yet another built-in mechanism for delay.

- **If they're so overworked, why don't they just approve my claim?** Suppose you had this person's job. What kind of impression would you make on your employer if you "rubber-stamped" everything that came across your desk?

It's a little-known fact that most independents get paid more for higher claim estimates. But insurance company examiners know all about this state of affairs, and they are inclined to compensate for it. In fact, they are trained and dedicated to "correcting" adjusters who are "padding" estimates for a higher fee. There's not only a built-in mechanism for delay; there's a built in incentive for skepticism about the dollar figures associated with claim estimates.

How deep does that skepticism run? Consider this: I recently spoke with an independent adjuster who complained that when his estimate is adjusted down, he only gets compensated based on the amount actually paid on the claim. If the claim is later *re-adjusted,* and the policyholder is eventually paid exactly what the independent initially requested, the independent adjuster still does not get paid what he would have been paid if his initial estimate had been accepted!

By the way, after this happens a few times, how long do you think it's going to take the independent adjuster to realize that he or she might as well just write the claim estimate for the (low) amount the insurance company is going to accept, and save the time and aggravation of writing the estimate for the (higher) amount that it *should* be written for?

• **What happens if the adjuster gets my claim kicked back to him or her?** There is additional delay. The adjuster now gets it back in his or her system. The adjuster has to find time to look at the file again to see what the examiner had a problem with; and then the adjuster has to try to resolve the problem, which might require another inspection. That means another trip through the adjuster's to-do list, probably a lengthy trip. And then, of course, your claim may require additional photographs, additional documentation, and additional phone calls. It is definitely going to require additional time.

• **Cut to the chase. How long is it going to take for me to get a check I can actually cash – a check that comes close to covering the valid claims I have?** That's the big question, of course. Assuming that the case does not end up in litigation, count on six months to a year before you get your money if you're trying to do this on your own. To be sure, some people complete the process in just a few months. There are three possible reasons for this. *One:* They're not getting all they're entitled to. *Two:* They're very, very lucky. *Three:* They're working with someone who knows the system quite well.

• **What if my claim is still disputed after a year or so?** It happens. In that case, you are probably headed to court (or should be), and can count on another two to three years before the claim is resolved by litigation. The insurance companies also know this, and they are not particularly worried about the time factor. It seems there is simply not any meaningful incentive for them to wrap the process up any more quickly. In fact, just the opposite seems to be the case. The longer the delay, the more likely it is that policyholders will either walk away from their claims altogether, or at least walk away with less than they have coming. It's my experience that most people simply don't realize how badly they've been underpaid, or have no idea how to dispute the claim, or are too mentally exhausted to bother anymore.

Why would you do that to yourself?

• **Would working with a public adjuster be likely to reduce the delays?** The answer is almost certainly "yes." A qualified public adjuster knows how the bureaucracy works (or rather, *doesn't* work). A qualified public adjuster knows what, if anything, can be done to expedite any part of the "holding pattern." An additional benefit, of course, is that the public adjuster isn't emotionally involved to the same degree that you are, which means he or she may simply be less shocked, burnt out, and/or furious about the delays than you are.

Again, a cynical man might wonder whether the insurance companies *count* on the policyholder's losing sleep – and initiative – over the extraordinary delays associated with getting the money they are owed.

- **Does pursuing a claim without outside help really burn policyholders out?** Definitely. I've seen it time and time again. After a certain amount of time, people have spent so much time and psychological energy on this problem they just cannot face it any more. The months go by, and people simply give up on believing that they can affect the outcome. So they take what they're offered -- or, to be more accurate, accept that they haven't been given what they deserve -- and try to move on with their lives. *That costs them money that they have coming to them.* Here's the moral of the story: You'd work with an attorney to handle serious legal problems. You should work with a public adjuster to handle serious insurance problems.

Unfortunately, delay is not the only problem you are likely to encounter when dealing with an insurance company after a hurricane, fire, flood, or other insured loss. You'll also have to deal with denial – quite possibly the most powerful weapon in the insurance industry's arsenal.

XI: In Denial

IF YOU'VE ENDURED delays on that mind-boggling scale, you might think that the system would finally start to work in your favor. For a large portion of the base of insurance policyholders, however, there is an unexpected and unpleasant surprise waiting when they finally hear back about the status of their claim: The insurance company **denies** some or all of the compensation the policyholder expected after the disaster.

Denial is one of the most potent tools at the insurance industry's disposal. Because most policyholders do not know the system as well as the insurance companies do, they either go along with the insurance company's decision, or fail to challenge it in an effective way.

Over the next few chapters, I'll show you how the insurance industry can use your lack of knowledge to make the process of denial work in their favor, not yours.

Even if you think you are willing to endure the surrealistic delays, you may still find yourself in a cold, dark, and confusing place ...

... the Denial Zone.

Q&A: What will happen

• **Why should I be so concerned about this "denial" business? My agent said I had an "all-risk" policy.** Buying such a policy does not, in the real world, protect you from having some or all of your claim denied.

The risks of an "all-risk" policy.

• **Realistically, what are the odds that the insurance company will deny some or all of my claim?** Depending on the type of loss, the odds could be very strong. They are certainly higher than most policyholders imagine when they buy a policy (especially an "all-risk" policy) or file a claim after a fire, flood, or other disaster.

• *Why* **is there such a strong chance of having my claim denied if I have an "all risk" policy?** This is a huge question, one that's very similar to the questions frustrated policyholders ask me when they get bad news from the insurance adjuster. Most policyholders are *extremely* surprised when they get word that all or part of a claim has been denied. I can tell you that they, too, want to know "why" such an outcome is possible. The short answer is that the insurance company probably didn't broadcast what the policy *didn't* cover when you bought it. The longer answer has to do with what they *really* meant when they sold you that so-called "all-risk" policy. Let's delve into that longer answer now.

- **Isn't an "all-risk" policy meant to protect me against all risks?** Alas, no. In most cases, it's actually *structured* to exclude certain risks, despite its name. Back when you bought your policy, the insurance agent was trying to sell you on a certain policy. Remember that?

Well, it's tough to sell a policy by broadcasting to the prospective buyer that Situation A is not covered, and Situation B is only covered in a certain very narrow way, and Situation C is covered only if Situation D is not in play. So the agent will generally say something like, "This is an all-risk policy that generally covers you for all risks, subject to certain limitations and exclusions."

Did you notice what just happened? The most important information sped by you. It hurtled past in that innocent-sounding word "generally," and then it sped by again in the little addition at the end of the sentence: "limitations and exclusions." (Or whatever similar language the insurance agent might decide to use; there are a lot of ways of sidestepping the question of what "all-risk" actually means.)

However agents decide to phrase this part about the exclusions during their discussions with you, they usually do not go into too much detail about what the exclusions *are*. In fact, in the average policy, there are pages and pages of exclusions and limitations. (A recent trend in hurricane policies is particularly troubling: the items that are usually damaged *first* and *most* are, in many cases, not covered at all!)

As the insurance industry is no doubt aware, members of the general public simply do not understand what's in all those dense pages of type. In fact, most people do not even attempt to read the policies in the first place. It's hard to avoid the conclusion that the industry counts on consumer ignorance about the policies they're buying.

• **How is that different from lying to me about what the policy actually covers?** I'm not an attorney, so I can't answer that, but I can tell you that the agent and the insurance company would, if you accused them of lying, probably point to the fact that you failed to read or understand the vast oceans of complex text that outlined all the exclusions in your policy. So to the industry (and, as a general rule, to a court of law) it's not lying, because they gave you the fine print. You simply didn't take the time to read or understand it. Good thing, too, because according to people who know much more about the law than I do, lying to you about what the policy actually covered would be fraud, which is a very serious matter.

• **Okay. How is what you're describing different from** *misleading* **me about what the policy actually covers?** No comment.

• **What kind of things am I, the policyholder, likely to think** *are* **covered ... that actually** *aren't?* The answer could fill another book this size. Just as a preliminary summary, though ... and to help you get your head around the magnitude of the gap that usually exists between what people assume is covered and what is *in fact* covered ... here's a thumbnail sketch of some of the "surprises" waiting for property owners after a disaster.

Assume there has been a hurricane in a given area. I can tell you with certainty that, at some point, there are going to be property owners who say ...

o   *"I thought my policy covered things like trees and lawns for hurricanes."* Almost never, even though these are typically among the first things that are badly damaged in a windstorm. Result: Denial!

o   *"I thought my policy covered fences damaged during a hurricane."* Ditto. More and more, fences are not covered in the event of damage by a hurricane. Note: restoring fencing to a property is usually extremely expensive. Result: Denial!

o   *"I thought my policy covered exterior paint."* Normally, yes, but many companies no longer cover this for hurricanes, even though exterior paint is very vulnerable in windstorms.

o   *"I thought my policy covered swimming pools and out buildings."* Again, it *usually* does, but it may *not* for a hurricane. Result: Ridiculously expensive denial!

o   And here's the big one: *"I thought I didn't need flood insurance!"* Sometimes people are told this by an insurance company. Sometimes they're told this by a mortgage company. However it happens; if homeowners believe it, the result can be an extremely unpleasant and costly surprise: Denial!

• **What was that about flood insurance and denial of my claim?** This question requires a detailed answer. You'll find it in the next chapter. We're about to discuss one of the most controversial and, for policyholders, infuriating corners of the *Denial Zone*: the misty region where wind meets water.

XII: Denial – Wind And Water

THERE'S AN OLD saying: "Denial is more than just the name of a river in Egypt." For consumers of property insurance, though, the joke has a cruel, updated variation: Denial is the name of a strategy insurance companies seem to use to avoid paying for the damage *caused* by rivers (among many other things).

In this chapter, we'll see how surprisingly indifferent the insurance industry is to a big problem – namely, that so many consumers believe, wrongly, either a) that their policies protect them against damage from floods, or b) that their property is not at a significant risk for flood damage.

Before we go any further, please understand one very important thing:

Insurance companies don't pay flood claims.

In case you just fell down from shock, and are now returning to consciousness with limited capacity, let me say it once again. *Insurance companies do not pay for flood claims*. Flood claims are ultimately paid by the Federal Government. If you have flood insurance, that's who you really bought it from: the government. The insurance companies simply adjust the losses. The handling standards are strict, and if the insurance companies mess up (i.e., overpay), they have to pay the money they overpaid policyholders back to Uncle Sam. (This leads us to an interesting side question: If the insurance company is going to err on a flood claim, can you guess which way they are going to lean?)

This situation is something that should concern you, since the reality of damage from flooding is looking like something more of us are going to have to prepare for in the coming years. According to the web site *World View of Global Warming*, "Meteorologists already see an increase in severity of storms, rainfall, and floods ..." They go on to observe that "These anomalies from what we think is 'normal' are expected to continue around the world."

Regardless of your stance on global warming (and its potential causes), regardless of what you believe, or don't believe, about natural weather cycles, the moral of the story is the same: *Think.* If you think you're not likely to be affected by a flood ... think again. If you think your homeowner's policy covers you against flood damage ... think again. I have personally witnessed the tragedy of property owners being without flood insurance. You don't want any part of it.

Q&A: What will happen

- **I don't think I need to read this chapter. If I was told by someone I trust that I didn't need flood insurance, doesn't that pretty much end the discussion?** No. People are told all the time -- by insurance companies, attorneys, or occasionally by representatives of mortgage companies or other "experts" -- that they have no need for flood insurance. All too often, this advice is simply incorrect. Sometimes what they say (or *mean* to say) is, "You are not *required* to carry flood insurance." That is *not* the same as your not *needing* it.

- **How would that bad advice affect me?** Let's say that your home is covered for wind damage, but *not* covered sufficiently for flood damage – because some "expert" told you that it wasn't 'required', because you didn't buy the right level of coverage, or because you thought, incorrectly, that flood damage was included in your homeowners' policy. And let's say a hurricane tears through your neighborhood. Let's say that the wind from the hurricane rips the roof off your house – followed, of course, by torrential rain, and then by a flood. (That's the sequence of events we all remember from Hurricane Katrina in 2005.)

When your insurance company reviews the claim, it's quite possible that it could deny all payment, on the argument that the damage to your house was caused, not by wind, but by flood.

Read that again.
It's important.

When your insurance company reviews the claim, it's quite possible that it could deny all payment, on the argument that the damage to your house was caused, not by wind, but by flood.

• Wait -- what if I've got an eyewitness who will swear that he saw the wind rip the roof off my house. Is it still possible that the insurance company could deny my claim for wind damage? Yes.

• Is that a hypothetical example, or is this something you actually know for sure that someone has experienced? It's not hypothetical. It actually happened to a neighbor of one of my clients. The existence of the eyewitness made no difference whatsoever to the insurance company's decision.

Again: consider the insurance company your adversary.

Ponder that example for a minute. What are the odds against someone actually *seeing* your roof get torn off, before the floods come? Yet for some companies, that's still not enough!

• **What exactly do insurance companies expect to get as proof of wind damage?** Well, my personal view is that they don't really *want* to see evidence in this situation. It's not like they launch a huge investigation to find out exactly what took place in your neighborhood: "Hmm … you appear to have a point here, Mr. Policyholder. Let's get to the bottom of this. Was it wind, or was it water? XYZ Insurance has an obligation to set the record straight once and for all!" That's not the kind of discussion you're going to hear. For the purposes of establishing their own responsibility (or *lack* of responsibility) for wind damages, the insurance companies *appear* to expect homeowners to have video cameras trained on their homes twenty-four hours a day, seven days a week, so as to record actual damage from windstorms *as that damage occurs.* As a practical matter, that's about what you would have to be prepared to provide them. If you *don't* have tangible proof of this kind – proof demonstrating beyond a shadow of a doubt the precise nature of the damage your property sustained – then it's entirely possible that the insurance company could choose to deny your claim. In the aftermath of a hurricane, they're likely to insist that water caused the damage in question, not wind … when they're talking to people who don't have flood insurance.

• **Is that kind of nitpicking out of line?** The attorney general of the state of Mississippi seemed to think so. In the aftermath of Hurricane Katrina, he took insurance companies to court. In Mississippi (and indeed in many other corners of our nation), it seems that a huge number of homeowners don't have, or can't get, adequate flood insurance on their homes, and are thus ill-equipped to respond to the denial games that insurance companies play after major natural disasters.

What you say can - and will - be used against you.

Very often, in a hurricane, a home suffers significant wind damage, but the evidence of that damage is masked or obstructed by a later flood.

This leads to a very dangerous situation.

I am not talking about the *physical* dangers now present within the property itself. I am talking, instead, about danger that's built into the system, financial danger for policyholders who are unfamiliar with the way the claims systems operate. I am talking about the dangers that confront those who are unwise enough to describe damage to an adjuster.

I can't count the number of times that insurance consumers made their position worse by describing to an adjuster, over the phone, the damage that was most vivid in their own minds. "The place is completely flooded!" "We're up to our ankles in water!" "There's extensive water damage!"

It all seems relevant. It all seems accurate. It all seems important. The damage from water is what has taken over the policyholder's world.

All too often, though, talking about it means *you lose!*

Think about this hypothetical situation for a moment: A hurricane has ripped the roof off your house. You're covered for that. You're now talking to an adjuster on your cell phone. Your home's primary coverage is for wind damage. But what have you just told the adjuster? *That you've got flood damage!* Game over!

• **Yeah, but that's a stressful situation. How can you expect policyholders to remember how important it is to watch what they say to an adjuster?** Let me answer that question by posing another: If you're in a perilous legal situation, which is equally stressful, would you talk to the prosecuting attorney on your own, or would you demand that your attorney be present? Step one, which should be obvious to you by now, is simply *not to talk to the adjuster*, but to delegate the job of talking to the adjuster to someone like me. Remember, the adjuster works *for* the insurance company. It's obviously easier for an adjuster to deny a claim than to do the work necessary to actually estimate one. If you say the words, "We're up to our ankles in water!" all the adjuster has to do is jot down the words "flood damage," and – if you're not covered for flood damage – voila! There's one less item on the to-do list!

Here's another example. Let's say that, five years ago, when you bought your home, you were advised by someone you trusted that you "didn't need" flood insurance. And let's say that, last week, your plumbing was damaged during a natural disaster of some kind: the pipes burst, and water leaked into your basement. When you finally get the adjuster on the phone, it would be quite natural for you to describe your home as "flooded." After all, there's standing water in the basement. But when that overworked adjuster hears that "F" word, his ears perk up, and two words start running through his mind, over and over and over again: "Not covered ... not covered ... not covered ..." *No matter what else you think is happening in the conversation, that's all the adjuster is going to be thinking: "Not covered."* And you know what else? Those two ominous words are likely to be followed by two *more* silent words you wouldn't like if you heard them: *"Easy close ... easy close ... easy close ..."* That means the adjuster is going to get credit, and quite possibly payment, for "closing" a file – yours – without having to do any real work. This is just one example of dozens I could give you that would show how a single thoughtless word – like "flooded" – can make your life absolutely miserable when you say it out loud to an adjuster.

• **What's the bottom line here?** If you get nothing else from this book, *get this:* Just as you wouldn't be well advised to talk directly to the IRS if you were being audited, and just as you wouldn't be well advised to talk directly to the D.A. if you were falsely charged with a crime, **you wouldn't be well advised to talk directly to the adjuster or the insurance company when a disaster damages or destroys your home.**

Don't risk it.
Get help!

In the first case, I would suggest retaining a CPA or other qualified tax professional. In the second, I would suggest retaining a lawyer. In the third, I would suggest retaining a public adjuster, and letting me, or someone like me, talk to the insurance company and their adjuster on your behalf.

Or think of it this way:

Let's say you know very little about cars, and let's say that, after a routine tune-up, the mechanic down the street informs you that your auto "needs a lot of work." Which of the following options would you rather choose?

o   Tell the mechanic to go ahead and get started, do whatever is necessary, and mail you the bill, whatever it turns out to be?

o   Or B), arrange for a car expert to meet with the mechanic, evaluate the situation on your behalf, and make absolutely sure you don't pay any more than you really need to?

Of course, you'd choose option B. We all would. **It's the same with insurance claims, especially those related to wind and water. You want an expert on your side.**

• **Where can I find out more about flood insurance?** Visit this web site right now: **www.floodsmart.gov**

• **What else should I know about this?** Let me share one more true story with you before we move on. A woman I'll call Mary had a condominium that was destroyed in a hurricane.

Luckily for her -- she thought -- she had *both* flood insurance (via Company X, but ultimately from the federal government) *and* wind insurance (via Company Y). I know what you're thinking, "With both policies in place, she must certainly have gotten paid something– at least by *one* of the carriers."

Wrong! By "co-adjusting" the two separate losses, the adjusters (and their respective insurance companies) determined that her situation *just happened* to fall into the tiniest of cracks between the two policies.

By a remarkable coincidence – are you keeping track of all these coincidences? – that crevice where her unique situation landed prevented the carriers from making payment on *either* claim!

Again: Don't risk it.
Get the help you need to deal with complex insurance challenges!

Keep reading!

We're about to learn about the dynamics of denial itself…and how the insurance industry has turned it into a force to be reckoned with, a force that *no* individual policyholder without significant training can realistically expect to overcome.

XIII: The Dynamics Of Denial

THE SAD TRUTH is, in far too many cases, the Powers That Be can categorize your loss in any way they see fit ... and then deny all or part of your claim. And the Powers That Be are, in all likelihood, far better at this categorizing-and-denying dynamic than you are at challenging it.

They are better at categorizing-and-denying than you are at challenging them.

A dynamic is, literally, something in motion – and that is exactly what you're going to feel like you're dealing with when you deal with this strategy: a moving target. You will have been under the impression that you were talking about one thing, and suddenly you'll get word from on high that, all along, you were really talking about something else ... something that the insurance company, by a remarkable coincidence, has no responsibility for.

One word for this process is "dynamic" – but another word, I think, might be "game." And just like in Las Vegas, it's a game that the House (in this case, your insurance company) will usually win.

Q&A: What you should know

• **Does this categorize-and-deny game affect all socioeconomic groups equally?** No. In my opinion, lower-income policyholders are much more likely to be adversely affected by what insurance companies do in terms of denial.

After just about any kind of disaster, there is a percentage of people in virtually any community whose claim will be denied by their insurers on the pretext that their home maintenance was poor. **This group is almost always disproportionately poor, disproportionately underexposed to post-high-school education, and disproportionately likely to belong to a minority group.**

In other words, there are certain neighborhoods in a community where a home may not have been painted for a while, and a door may not have been fixed that should have been fixed. In these homeowners' policies, there are, almost always, innocent-sounding "maintenance" and "wear and tear" exclusions. It seems fair enough: the insurance company isn't responsible for compensating for normal wear and tear; the homeowner has an obligation to maintain the property. Watch what happens, though. After a disaster or other claim, and after a nightmare of delay and bureaucratic runarounds, the homeowner finally meets with an adjuster. Can you guess what happens next? The adjuster simply decides that he or she can't (or won't) separate the damage of the disaster from the normal wear and tear of a home that happens to be occupied by people who can't afford a full-time housekeeping and repair staff.

Without a public adjuster, these people may have their claims denied in part or in full, on the grounds that they have failed to maintain their homes properly.

Look at it again:

> **"You didn't paint for a while. That means _you must not be covered for a hurricane,_ because your poor maintenance makes it impossible for me to say for sure that a hurricane caused this damage."**

With a public insurance adjuster working on their side, these policyholders are, in my experience, far more likely to receive a fair settlement from the insurance company … even if there _is_ physical evidence that they could, in a perfect world, have maintained their homes a little better.

• **Why do adjusters do this kind of thing? Are they really "out to get" homeowners and deny as many claims as possible?** It's more complicated than that. There are a lot of reasons adjusters may end up denying some or all of your claim. Part of it, perhaps, is simple laziness. (In the example I just mentioned, the wear-and-tear and maintenance issue, an adjuster may spot a few home-repair problems and decide that it's simply easier to deny the whole claim than to do the work necessary to distinguish water damage from over-looked carpentry projects.)

Other issues might be inexperience, a ridiculously over-stacked schedule, or a subtle series of messages from the insurance company to whom they are reporting. Let me be clear: I believe that at the outset of their work with the insurance company, adjusters are told to pay every valid claim. But that's a message that might only get sent once or twice during the adjuster's relationship with the insurer. Far more potent, over time, are the *daily* messages an adjuster receives. Even assuming that adjusters are never told (directly) to deny valid claims, they are given little "raps on the knuckles," little messages from upstairs: "You did this wrong, you did that wrong, you paid too much here, you overlapped there." It only takes a few weeks for these messages to land. Adjusters, of course, do not want to continue to go through the process of getting their knuckles rapped. They start figuring out for themselves what the insurance company (really) wants. And so, by the way, do the engineers, repair and restoration firms and other 'experts' sent out by the insurance company to "help" you deal with your situation. I'll have more to say about these people later on in the book, but for now, let me just leave you with this hint: If the insurance company sent them, don't expect them to have your best interests in mind, even if you *are* the one paying them.

• **What else can I expect as an excuse for denial of all or part of my claim?** Plenty. The insurance company may "misread" a critical definition of a word within your policy. Result: Denial. Or: The insurance company may declare that your going on vacation (or having some other reason for leaving the property for a period) invalidated your policy. Result: Denial. Or: The insurance company may choose to fixate on a clause in your policy that's designed to remove responsibility for coverage in situation X – and they may try to apply that clause to situation Y, which has only the remotest connection to situation X. Result: Denial. *Unless you are working with someone like me.*

For instance, an insurance company once tried to deny coverage to one of my clients on the basis of a leak in the roof of the property. They had fixated on the word "leak" in the homeowner's policy exclusion. As it happened, though, that kind of "leak" wasn't what justified the exclusion used. The relevant section of the policy talked about *a repeated leak in a shower area.* The leak had to be located specifically in the area of the shower for the denial to stick --- and that was not what had happened at all. But that didn't stop the insurance company from selecting a very tiny portion of that exclusion to quote in support of their denial of coverage. Result : Denial if you're *not* working with someone like me; no denial if you *are* working with someone like me. (Fortunately, my client was!)

These are the kinds of problems that can be overcome if you use a qualified public adjuster. All are very difficult to spot – and thus difficult to challenge – if you're unfamiliar with the language of insurance policies or the dynamics of denial.

At the risk of being blunt, let me put this another way:

The company knows what it's doing. You don't.

You get the picture by now. It's in your best interests to work with someone who knows as much about the dynamics of denial as the insurance company does!

In the next section of this book, we'll look at the third major weapon in the insurance company's arsenal – their remarkable skill at **deflecting responsibility** for actually paying you what you are owed.

XIV: The Deflection Game

EVEN IF YOU endure all the delays, and even if you somehow work your way through the labyrinth of denials, the insurance industry may well have one more coincidence up its sleeve. This coincidence catches a lot of insurance consumers by surprise. It often contributes to the exasperated, exhausted homeowner's conclusion that it's better to give up, settle for what they can get, and perhaps accept dimes, nickels, or even pennies on the dollars they are actually owed.

The coincidence is known as deflection, and it's what happens when the insurance company finds reasons to avoid paying you money that you actually have coming on your claim. Although listed last in this book, deflection can be encountered at any time during the claim.

In this chapter, I'll give you a broad overview of the "deflection game"; in the chapters that follow, we'll look at how the game is actually played to the detriment of you, the policyholder.

Like the coincidences mentioned in previous chapters, this one requires the help of a professional if you want to stand the barest chance of getting all you are owed. All too often, though, this is a game that non-professionals lose ... simply because they **don't realize they're playing in the first place.**

Q&A: What you should know

• **What, exactly, does the "deflection game" involve?** It involves the insurance company finding ways to avoid giving a direct, truthful answer to what would seem to be a fairly basic question: "Who has the moral and legal responsibility to make sure that my legitimate claim is paid in full, promptly and to my complete satisfaction?"

• **Isn't that obvious? Doesn't the insurance company itself have the obligation to pay the claim?** That answer may perhaps seem obvious to the policyholder, but sometimes it's *not* all that obvious to an insurance company with a multitude of adjusters, engineers, restoration companies, attorneys, insurers, re-insurers, and third-party administrators at its disposal. There are so many cases of insurance companies dodging this issue that I can't really do justice to the topic in a book of this size. I can say, though, that it seems the legal system has finally begun to catch up with a few of the worst offenders.

• **What kinds of cases are we talking about?** In Ohio, a jury held that a life insurance and disability management services company was guilty of breach of insurance contract; the jury awarded the plaintiffs $429,400 in compensatory damages for nonpayment of claims. But that wasn't all. The jury also found the insurance company guilty of bad faith insurance practices, and mandated an award of $1,130,000 to the plaintiffs. **They coupled this with a whopping punitive damages award of $3 million.**

Documents from the case give some sense of the elaborate lengths to which some companies will go to avoid paying people the money they are owed. This particular insurance company used a third party administrator, and an affiliate re-insurer (which was also a 40% owner of the third party administrator) to combine their efforts in an **illegal scheme to avoid paying completely legitimate claims.**

The scheme involved a whole host of complex accounting maneuvers, as well as false information that was submitted to an insurance commission. Now, I realize that, at this point, you may be having some difficulty getting your head around all this. That's because a) such cases are pretty complicated and b) you're probably still thinking of insurance companies as responsible businesses with an obligation to take care of their customers over the long term. **All too often, it seems they're simply *not* very responsible, and *not* thinking about the interests of their customers in any timeframe, short or long.**

• **Are there other cases like that Ohio case you mentioned?** Plenty. Many have a disturbing, and all-too-common, theme – the insurance company says that **paying you is actually someone else's responsibility.**

But the "someone else" either never follows through or only partially follows through on its obligation to you. Or they say that the other party's report or advice "prevents" them from paying you (as if they can't override the opinion of an outside party). I've personally seen this happen many, many times.

- **Do all of these cases wind up in court?** No. In my opinion, very few of the cases that could go to court ever get there, and most policyholders in these situations do not get the impartial hearing they deserve.

- **Why not?** Because many individual policyholders simply can't tolerate the idea of wandering into another bureaucratic maze with no clear outcome that they can see benefiting them in the near future. (As we all know, going to court can be a long, expensive process.) After all the delays, after all the denials, many people are simply sick of the process of trying to get the insurance company to pay up. They either take whatever crumbs they've already been tossed, settle prior to trial, or give up altogether. As I've suggested elsewhere in this book, I suspect a fair number of people chose one of these three options in an effort to preserve their own sanity.

It's not really that surprising that most of these situations don't land in a courtroom. By the time most people start thinking about lawsuits, they've already been battling the insurance company for a year or more. Then they are told the lawsuit will probably take another two to three years! Be honest. What would you do? Sometimes, when people find themselves caught in the "deflection game," they'll give just about anything to be done with the process.

- **Are these "deflection" situations isolated cases?** If you ask representatives of the insurance industry, the answer will be an immediate "Yes." If you ask Elliot Spitzer, former New York Attorney General, and current Governor of the State of New York, he'd offer a somewhat different assessment of the situation.

• **What did Spitzer have to say about this?** In a lawsuit, Mr. Spitzer accused major insurance companies of "fraud, bid-rigging, and antitrust violations," and charged some of the biggest players in the game with fleecing their customers. Spitzer warned that the American insurance industry "needs to take a long, hard look at itself," and suggested that "if the practices identified in our suit are as widespread as they appear to be, then the industry's fundamental business model needs major corrective action and reform." He went on to note that "there is simply no responsible argument for a system that rigs bids, stifles competition and cheats customers." Mr. Spitzer's investigation and lawsuit focused first on corporate customers, but specifically included individual consumers as being among those victimized by industry practices. His press release was entitled "Investigation Reveals Widespread Corruption In Insurance Industry."

• **Isn't the legal system supposed to correct problems like this?** In theory, yes. And there are some encouraging signs. A 2007 DecisionQuest poll of practicing attorneys found 75% of respondents would now expect jurors to agree with the sentiment that insurance companies "would do anything to avoid paying even legitimate claims." That's refreshing evidence of reality-based thinking within the halls of justice. But most of these cases, as we have seen, never reach a jury.

For your own protection and economic well-being, it may be wisest to *stop* thinking of insurance companies in terms of your friendly neighborhood insurance agent, and *start* thinking of insurance companies as resembling the people who ran their firms into the ground by setting up a nearly-incomprehensible maze of wholly-owned, partially-owned, and "affiliated" companies ... companies whose relationship with one another seemed to require an advanced degree.

I realize that sounds like a harsh assessment. But the irresponsible use of deflection warrants it, in my view. Let me give you a brief example that may help you understand why I feel as I do about this.

Think of a big insurance company. Let's call it Baseball, Mom, and Apple Pie Insurance – BMAPI for short. BMAPI's motto is , "Faithful and friendly, during good times and bad." It has an expensive ad campaign that features gorgeous sunsets, adorable puppy dogs, and happy policyholders who dearly love and respect their local BMAPI agent.

Now, if BMAPI handles, say, 1.5 million claims in a year, and then deflects – sorry, "saves" – just *$300* on each claim, that adds up to nearly **five hundred million dollars** more for BMAPI to keep for itself and invest as it sees fit.

Yes. Nearly *half a billion* dollars.

Follow me on this next part, because it's extremely important.

The number I just used to get to roughly half a billion dollars of extra income for BMAPI was, you will recall, *three hundred dollars* of, shall we say, "savings." Now, you might well ask: How realistic is that figure I just used? Is three hundred dollars a valid number -- or a dubious number? Hear me, please, when I tell you that my typical additional recoveries – that is, the money I get the insurance company to agree to pay in valid claims over and above what it had already agreed to pay out – is not in the *hundreds* of dollars.

It's in the *thousands* of dollars. That's in my *average* case.

Read it again.

Ponder that, please. Not three hundred dollars per case. *Thousands* of dollars per case. And that's not the exception to the rule. That's what *usually* happens.

Deflection happens. Deflection is real!

For more information on bad faith insurance issues, please take the time to visit this web site:

www.badfaithinsurance.org

-- or just do a Google search with the words "bad faith" along with the name of your own "friendly and faithful" insurance company, and see what kind of ugliness pops up. You may be surprised.

In the next chapter, we'll get some more clarity on exactly how the "deflection game" is likely to be played in your world.

XV: Basic Deflection

IN THE PREVIOUS CHAPTER, I gave you an overview of the insurance industry's third big coincidence – deflection.

When you encounter this event, which can come about at any point in the process, you'll learn that the industry is quite adept at shifting responsibility for taking action on a valid claim to some other organization, entity, or person. In this chapter, we'll get a close look at some of the simpler methods that the industry has established over the years for deflecting important questions. What follows is a thumbnail sketch of what might be called "low-level" or "basic" deflection. (We'll look at some of the more advanced strategies the industry can put into play in the next chapter.)

Q&A: What you should know

• **How does the insurance industry make deflection work in its favor at the most basic level?** By taking full advantage of the coincidence of incompetence among the very people it hires as adjusters and other third-party representatives.

I can't tell you how many times policyholders have had an experience like the following:

> o *Call the insurance company. Get a recording with another number to call.*

o *Call the number (disaster call center). Hold for extended period. Get disconnected.*

o *Call the call center repeatedly. Hold for extended period. Find out it wasn't the call center that you wanted to talk to.*

o *Get adjuster's number to call.*

o *Call the adjuster. Fail to get a response.*

o *Call the adjuster. Fail to get a response.*

o *Call the adjuster several more times. Finally, get some unsatisfying response.*

o *Call the adjuster. Fail to get any response, even an unsatisfying one.*

o *Wait absurd amount of time. After losing all patience with the adjuster, call the insurance company to complain.*

o *Upon reaching the insurance company, hear something like the following: "We've had problems with that adjuster – he's no longer working for us. We've assigned someone else to your claim."*

o *And so on.*

I know it sounds absurd, but you can rest assured that this kind of thing really happens. Here is an actual call center conversation sent to me by a client:

Policyholder: "Hello, I'm calling about my claim."

Insurance company: "The phone number for the claims department is no longer being answered by the claims department."

Policyholder: "Why?"

Insurance company: "The claims department is not taking calls because they are too busy. You can leave a message and someone will call you back."

Policyholder: "When?"

Insurance company: "We can't say, because they are just too busy."

Policyholder: "Is there a number I can call for the claims department?"

Insurance company: "Yes, the number you just called."

Policyholder: "But you said you were not the claims department."

Insurance company: "Yes, that's correct.. Is there anything else I can help you with?"

Policyholder: "Well, I'm not sure, since you haven't helped me at all."

Notice that, because the call center person or adjuster is often an independent contractor, rather than a full-time employee, the insurance company itself is very often not "at fault" for anything -- beyond selecting a poor contractor. "Besides," they will tell you, "this was a major catastrophe." As if your home being in ruins wasn't a good enough hint.

Note, too, the cumulative effect of this whole process, especially the insurance company's assurance that someone else is now on the case ... someone who will be equally hard to track down. The cumulative effect is to further exasperate and frustrate the policyholder. You're one step closer to giving up on the whole process. Once again, people within the industry are likely to say that such a turn of events is entirely coincidental and beyond their control. But this coincidence, too, endlessly repeated in the lives of thousands upon thousands of policyholders who have recently experienced a disaster or accident, happens to benefit the bottom line of the industry as a whole. **And all the while, the company can claim that the dereliction of duty is not their responsibility, but someone else's.**

• **Are "incompetent" adjusters the industry's only means of deflecting responsibility for taking action on a valid claim?** Not by a long shot. Think of it this way: if you wanted to go out hunting for bear, would you load only one bullet in your gun?

• **What other varieties of low-level deflection do policyholders have to contend with?** One of the most common is what I call the "Engineer's Deflection." In this shocking coincidence, the engineering firm the insurance company hires becomes the scapegoat. The insurance company will say that it has to arrange for the opinion of an outside expert – typically an engineering firm – to assess a specific damage to your property. Time will pass. The engineer will be identified. More time will pass. The engineer will show up to look at your property. The engineer will make an inspection, take some photographs and notes, and leave. More time will pass (usually a lot more time). The engineer will file a report with the insurance company. More time will pass.

Having analyzed the report, the insurance company will find something unusual, strange, or inadequate about an issue the engineer has raised, and will tell the adjuster about it. More time will pass.

The adjuster will inform you that his or her "hands are tied" – that the engineer has found a problem or inconsistency that keeps the adjuster from processing the claim in your favor.

In these situations, it's not at all uncommon for the adjuster to tell the homeowner something along the following lines: "In most cases where we encounter (storm damage/fire damage/whatever damage) like this, we pay the claim ... but in your situation, the engineer found (Strange Situation We Hardly Ever Encounter). I wish I could pay the claim, but the engineer's report won't let me."

What the adjuster won't tell you in this situation is that the same speech, with slight variations, has been delivered to countless other policyholders who trusted that insurance company, and paid that insurance company, to protect them against a certain risk.

- **Can the engineer really "tie the insurance company's hands" in this way?** Absolutely not. The engineering firm is not driving the process, and the engineer's report is not binding on the insurance company. It is one tool, and only one tool, the company uses to determine the cause, nature and extent of the damage to your property. A different engineering report from a different firm can (and often does) point toward a totally different conclusion. But the insurance company, and the adjuster it hires to represent it, often likes to pretend that a report from an engineer that "raises red flags" is like an edict from the U.S. Supreme Court.

Of course, it doesn't have to be an engineer. The entity "tying the insurance company's hands" can be a roofer, plumber, contractor, restoration company, weather service – the deflection list goes on and on.

- **Who else can the insurance company use as an agent of "low-level" deflection?** You.

- **Me?** Yes, you, the policyholder. In a lawsuit filed by Mississippi Attorney General Jim Hood, it was alleged that in the aftermath of Hurricane Katrina, and without drawing much attention to themselves, insurance industry representatives went around visiting homeowners and asked them to sign some (seemingly) routine paperwork before the adjuster could actually examine the property or pay for living expenses. Many of the homeowners, eager to get the wheels of the adjusting process moving, or out of desperation for the promise of financial assistance, simply signed these documents without reading them closely. Big mistake.

What the papers said was that the policyholders were

acknowledging that they were victims of flood damage (for which they were not covered) rather than hurricane damage (for which they were). Thus, the final responsibility for nonpayment of the claim shifted to the all-too-compliant policyholder. Who made this deflection possible? You did!

• **What's the moral of these horror stories?**   There are three big lessons to take away from these stories. First, and most important, get a public adjuster working for you just as soon as you suspect you may have to file a claim for damage to your property (or, at the very least, once you find your claim going sour). Second, refer all questions about engineers and engineering reports to your public adjuster. And third, never, ever sign anything because you think you're "supposed to" in order to get an insurance company adjuster to look at your property. There should never be any preliminary paperwork necessary to get an adjuster to assess damage to your home.

Turn the page to hear what basic deflection may sound like for *you*.

"We'd love to move this forward for you – but we can't. Somebody else is holding it up; somebody else stopped the process in its tracks."

That's "low-level" deflection. In the next chapter, you'll see some of the examples of *advanced* deflection from the insurance industry. They're even scarier.

XVI: Advanced Deflection

YOU NOW UNDERSTAND the basic principles behind what may well be the insurance industry's ultimate coincidence – deflection. As you may have noticed, it's pretty complicated. Unfortunately, the process now gets even more complex.

In addition to playing a kind of shell game involving you, the adjuster, and the engineering firm, the insurance company may bring *other* outsiders into the picture. When they do, the outcome, in far too many cases, is a game at a whole different level, a game that most policyholders can't understand, much less win. Again: Just like the gambling casino in Vegas or Atlantic City, certain industries tend to promote games that it knows the House will win. In this chapter, I'm going to share one example of the kind of "advanced" deflection game you may well find yourself up against after a major property loss.

Q&A: What you should know

• **What is "advanced" deflection on the part of the insurance industry?** It's deflection that uses a *separate company* that appears to be acting on behalf of the insurance company, but in your best interest.

- **Why "appears"?** Because, ultimately, the company may not be acting in your interest at all. Just like the insurance company, this company is best regarded as your adversary.

- **Can you give an example of this?** There are many examples, but perhaps the most dramatic involves special building contractors known as "preferred vendors." As the name implies, these companies are "preferred" contractors recommended by the insurance company following a loss. But you should understand *why* the insurance company "prefers" to use them. The insurance company uses them because they're cost-effective *from the insurance company's point of view*. From your point of view, though, there may well be very expensive problems.

- **How am I likely to come in contact with such a "preferred service provider"?** It's a distinct possibility, especially after a major natural disaster. (Keep in mind, though, that different insurance companies call these providers by different names.)

Here's how it might happen: Let's say your home has experienced significant water damage from a burst pipe, and your floor is ruined. The adjuster, or a representative of the insurance company, may say something like this: "We've got everything covered – you don't even have to look around for a contractor. We're going to send out a repair firm. They're on our preferred list. They'll handle everything. Just sign the paperwork they'll give you when they show up and give them your deductible." Those may not be the exact words you hear, but the gist of the message will probably be the same. "Don't worry, we'll take care of you." How convenient it all seems!

- **Then what happens?** The contractor shows up at your doorstep … and you probably make a huge mistake.

- **What mistake is that?** You imagine that the contractor is working *for the insurance company* to fix your floor. But in fact, the contractor is operating as an independent business. From a formal point of view, the contractor is now working for *you,* which means you, not the insurance company, are responsible for resolving any problems that arise.

- **Wouldn't that be true of any contractor I chose?** Yes.

- **Why is this relationship different?** Because even though the contractor is (technically) working for you, it's been *referred* by the insurance company. In other words, that's where it gets a good deal of its business from. So its priorities about things like quality, workmanship, timeliness, customer care, and even respect for your belongings may not be based on how happy you are with the job they do. Even though they may be *legally* working for you, some of these providers act as if the insurance company is the entity they're most interested in *keeping happy.* This can lead to some very unfortunate situations.

- **For instance?** In one case I worked on, the homeowner had sustained significant water damage. The contractor showed up at the homeowner's door, handed over some paperwork, and told the homeowner to "sign here." The homeowner signed and paid the deductible, under the impression that the insurance company was actually performing the repairs, and would hold the contractor accountable. **Not so!**

As it happened, the job took three weeks, not the three to

five days the homeowner had been promised. The quality of the work was slapdash, with paint splattered everywhere and sub-par finish work. And as if that weren't enough, the contractor placed all of the homeowner's furniture in a portable storage unit just outside the home … a portable storage unit that happened to have a *leak*.

Then the rain fell, but nobody knew that the furniture was being ruined. The family sustained thousands of dollars of additional losses to their furniture!

- **Which the insurance company covered, right?** No! The insurance company claimed that, because the homeowner had "signed here," the work of the contractor --- and the *oversights* of the contractor – were entirely the homeowner's responsibility! Once again, the insurance company's response was an unwelcome one: "It's not our responsibility." That's advanced deflection.

- **What did the contractor do?** It stonewalled, totally ignoring the homeowners.

- **How likely am I to be able to turn around a situation similar to that on my own, as an individual homeowner?** Not likely at all.

- **So did this homeowner lose out?** Fortunately, no. They came to me, and I was able to convince the insurance company to live up to its obligations.

- **What was the result?** The homeowners were compensated for the shoddy workmanship, the failure to live up to basic standards of professionalism, and the loss of their furniture. In the end, I secured a $47,000 settlement for them *over and above* the $25,000 the insurance company had initially paid to the contractor to do the work.

• **Are there other kinds of deflection I should watch out for?** Sure. Every claim is different, and the ways insurance companies are handling them (and introducing other parties into the mix) changes all the time, so we can't get into every type of deflection. But you get the idea.

It's real. It happens. It can happen to you.

XVII: The Top Ten Warning Signs That Your Insurer Is About To Make Your Life Miserable

IN THIS CHAPTER, you will find the top ten warning signs of problems on the horizon with your insurer.

Trouble on the horizon? Take action.

If you spot even one of these warning signs, you should call me immediately at 1-800-523-2589, or e-mail me at *Mark@GoldStarAdjusters.com* -- ASAP!

What you should watch out for

Warning Sign Number Ten: By phone or by form letter, the insurance company tells you something to the effect that "due to the large number of claims received," the process of resolving your claim will be delayed.

Here, remarkably, is something you can be absolutely sure your insurance company is telling the truth about. If they say your claim will be delayed, take it to the bank! Again, this is what *usually* happens in catastrophe situations. You will need professional guidance in this situation. ***Call me.***

Warning Sign Number Nine: Someone from a call center tells you that an adjuster "should be calling" within 24-48 hours.

The tip-off here is the call center, not the adjuster, is the one actually calling you. I wouldn't suggest taking off work to wait for that call. You are almost certainly in for a longer wait. Use the time wisely. ***Call me.***

Warning Sign Number Eight: The adjuster does not call when the call center indicated.

Surprise, surprise. This seems harmless enough at the time, but it's definitely not a good sign. You have now officially begun the process of risking your sanity. It's simply not worth it. Get someone else to take on the process of tracking this person down. ***Call me.***

Warning Sign Number Seven: The adjuster schedules the inspection of your home more than one week in advance.

Most policyholders don't realize that this is a clear indicator that they are *not* at the top of the list. No matter what you write down in the calendar, a time lag of more than one week before the inspection often translates as "You do not yet exist in my world." Not where you want to be! *Call me.*

Warning Sign Number Six: The adjuster cancels or misses the scheduled appointment.

Alas, this is quite common. It may signal any number of problems: the adjuster's lack of organization in the face of a surrealistically high workload, burnout, confusion, reassignment, firing, or even the adjuster's decision to go AWOL for one or more personal reasons. Of all of these, reassignment is probably the most likely reason for the failure to appear. In catastrophe situations, adjusters can be -- and are -- reassigned from area to area a number of times, creating high stress levels, epic burnout rates, and serious turnover. You very likely *won't* get any advance notice ahead of time about this reassignment. You are now at the mercy of the system. *Call me.*

Warning Sign Number Five: After inspecting your property, the adjuster advises you that the estimate will take more than ten to fourteen days to complete.

Big problems ahead. For a number of reasons, including but not limited to the inevitable failings of the human memory, estimates that are not completed within this time frame tend to feature significant mistakes. (Would you care to guess in whose favor those mistakes will probably lean?) This kind of "open time frame" also suggests that the adjuster is taking on more and more inspections … rather than completing work on the claims that have already been seen. This kind of delay may improve the adjuster's financial situation, thanks to the additional fees collected, but it probably won't do much for your own bank balance. *Call me.*

Warning Sign Number Four: There are long time lapses between calls, inspections, and your receipt of the adjuster's estimate.

Not what you had in mind. This is still more evidence that the adjuster is overworked, disorganized, improperly trained, improperly compensated, or a combination of all of the above. Don't try to fix these problems yourself; don't try to bulldoze your way through them. You can't. *Call me.*

Warning Sign Number Three: The adjuster tells you your file is being transferred to another adjuster or another unit.

Somehow, this file transfer rarely seems to work out well for the policyholder. In most situations, you won't like the new adjuster any more than you liked what was happening (or not happening) with the first adjuster. *Call me.*

Warning Sign Number Two: You receive voluminous requests for information.

Attempting to fulfill these voluminous requests will take you quite a long time. Some of the requested information will be impossible for you to supply. Some of it will be a little easier for you to track down. Some of the information you do pass along will not satisfy the Powers That Be. (You get the idea.) This kind of request is an indicator that someone in the bureaucracy "smells something fishy." You may not know what that something is, and, as a result, you almost certainly won't know whether you are hurting or helping your cause as you track down all of this data. *Call me.*

And the Number One warning sign that your insurer is about to make your life miserable ...

You get letters with ominous language that you've never seen before, like *"non-waiver"* or *"reservation of rights."* Most policyholders are confused and disoriented by this turn of events, and may even put off dealing with it because they don't know what to do. *This is what the insurer is hoping you will do.* In fact, when this happens, you should be thinking "denial," and you should be reaching out to a qualified public adjuster and preparing for battle.

If you're like ninety-seven out of one hundred of the policyholders I run into, you're simply not going to win this battle if you attempt to fight it on your own. *Call me.*

If even one of these things happen ...

... *contact me immediately.* Of course, you should also contact me in the case of later "warning signs" that suggest a major collapse of the process, like the insurer denying all or part of your claim, the insurer suggesting fraud on your part, or the insurer demanding that you (or someone else) be examined under oath.

Again: You wouldn't try to handle an important IRS, medical, or other significant issue without a professional. *Don't try to handle a major insurance issue without a professional on your side!*

Keep the information on the next page handy: clip it out and slip it into your wallet.

Mark Goldwich
Gold Star Adjusters, LLC.
www.GoldStarAdjusters.com
Mark@GoldStarAdjusters.com
1-800-523-2589

XVIII: Why I Did This

I WON'T TELL you the name of the insurance company I used to work for – I'll just tell you that it was a major player. Let's call the company I used to work for BigCo.

BigCo was really good at creating a sense of "welcoming culture" within the organization for its employees. When I started there in the late eighties, the company really seemed to offer a "family" atmosphere.

My landing a job at BigCo was quite a coup; BigCo was a "prestige" company, and competition to get in was fierce. They didn't really have to advertise for new hires. You usually had to know someone or be related to someone who worked at BigCo to get a job offer there. It was a good company to work for. There were lots of benefits.

Getting promoted to supervisor in under five years was another big accomplishment. Generally, you had to work there at least seven years before you could expect something like that. So I was on the fast track. I felt as if I were on top of the world. I was a company guy. I was all about BigCo.

A big change happened for me in 1996, though. That was when I became part of BigCo's newly developed national catastrophe program. I gave up my job as a local supervisor at BigCo. The new position required a lot of travel. Because I had taken the new job, I was now traveling around the country, staying at a seemingly endless series of hotels, and working very, very long hours. Twelve hour days were the minimum; six-day work weeks were the norm. I got a weekend off – as in two straight days at home – only every six weeks or so.

While working on the catastrophe team at BigCo, I began to see first-hand all the subtle ways the company manipulated the process to the disadvantage of policyholders. I began to notice how the words the company used pointed in one direction … but the actions we took tended to point in another, very different direction.

Working at disaster sites, strolling through the ruins of people's homes, was, for me, a sobering and humbling way to make a living. Supposedly, we were there to help. But often, I found us merely scurrying about trying to get just enough money into people's hands to keep complaints at a minimum. I saw too many "high-fives" among BigCo team members when a policyholder's claim was denied.

I also began to see that the "family culture" that BigCo took such pride in was more complex than I had imagined. It now had a darker side – you were part of the family *as long as* you did exactly what you were told, and *as long as* you accepted, without challenge, all the unspoken assumptions you were supposed to accept.

I now found myself face-to-face with those assumptions on a daily basis, and it was difficult for me to ignore their human costs. I realized that, to be "BigCo people," we had to buy into those assumptions but never, ever say them out loud, either internally or externally. I could no longer escape the conclusion that these assumptions were uprooting the lives of a very large number of our policyholders.

Some of these unspoken "BigCo Family" assumptions were:

- **Claims from consumers are likely to be inflated, if not fraudulent. Treat them that way.**

- **You can always find a reason to delay: request additional information; get better documentation; get clarification; say you have to investigate more fully; seek higher authority for whatever has to happen next.**

- **You can always find something to deny, reduce payment on, or limit.**

- **You can always find a way to deflect responsibility. Find someone or something else to blame for the situation the policyholder is facing.**

- **While you are doing these things, you must maintain, and endorse, the public position that BigCo is doing everything right, and is always out to give policyholders a fair shake. Regardless of how many policyholders complain to you about how they are treated, you must preserve the public image of BigCo as fair and responsible.**

These, I came to realize, were some of the dark secrets behind the "family culture" at BigCo. You were only part of the "family" if you agreed to conceal these basic working principles from the media, from the general public, and from policyholders.

It was time to get out.

I began a career as a public adjuster. Shortly after leaving BigCo and starting work in my new field, I was working in the Florida Panhandle with a retired Air Force veteran whom I'll call "Captain Charlie." He and his wife had been hit hard by Hurricane Ivan.

Captain Charlie's house had been devastated by Ivan's winds, as well as by eight to ten inches of flood water. His roof had been turned into a sieve, and there was major interior and exterior damage. The contents of his home had been ruined.

Captain Charlie's insurer gave him a shockingly low building-loss offer, and denied his claim for the contents of his home *entirely*.

In a preview of the dodge the insurance industry was to become infamous for a few years later with Hurricane Katrina, Captain Charlie's insurer told him that his entire claim for the personal contents of the home had been rejected because the home wasn't covered for flood damage. Guess what? Captain Charlie didn't have a flood policy.

The fact was, though, that much of what they denied could not have possibly been damaged by flood, since the objects in question were ten inches or more off the ground, and were directly underneath one of several gaping holes in a collapsed, storm-drenched ceiling.

It was an infuriating result -- one I knew I could improve for Captain Charlie.

Knowing the internal workings of companies like his as well as I did, I took it as my personal mission to win Captain Charlie a better settlement. He paid me nothing up front. (None of my clients pay me anything up front.)

He ended up getting over $39,000 that had originally been denied for contents of his home. I also secured additional payments on his home itself that totaled over $71,000; after you added everything up, it was over a hundred and ten thousand dollars.

I'll never forget the look on Captain Charlie's face when he got the news – over a hundred grand in additional payments from an insurer that had chosen to fight him tooth and nail, and had lost. I've never seen a man more grateful.

That was my first major victory against one of many BigCos running roughshod over the very lives of the policyholders who kept them in business. There were lots more victories to come.

Yours should be next!

Appendices

Appendix A: "They Want To Examine Me Under Oath!"

AN "EXAMINATION UNDER OATH" is what happens when the insurance company requires you to sit in front of *their* attorney (or attorneys) and a court reporter. It's about as much fun as it sounds. You may be interrogated for hours.

Should you do it?

Most policies require you to subject yourself to this whenever the insurance company "reasonably" requests that you do so. Failure to comply is usually grounds for full denial of the claim. Despite whatever the insurance company may say to the contrary, the aim here is almost certainly not "routine." If they want you to talk under oath, the company may want to get you on the record so you can be prosecuted for fraud. What they will tell you in this situation, though, will sound conciliatory, or even helpful to you. They may claim, for instance, that they "need additional information," to process your claim; or they may tell you they "want to get your side of the story," for the sake of thoroughness. Usually, they just say the policy requires you to appear if you want to pursue your claim. Many people are simply too intimidated to continue.

A big-name insurance company once told me that not only did my client have to appear for an examination under oath, but that *another* party had to appear and be subjected to an examination under oath as well. I was warned that, if my client could not get this other party to appear, her entire claim could be denied.

When we objected that the other party was not an insured, and that my client could not force the person in question to appear, the insurance company insisted that it had the power to demand that my client serve up the *mailman* if it concluded he could add something to their investigation of the claim. What's more, my client was also told that she would soon be arrested for insurance fraud if she continued with her claim.

In this case, some of the insurance company's threats turned out to be a bluff. My client did not have to answer questions under oath, was not prosecuted for fraud, and did not have to produce the mailman (or anyone else) for the insurance company to question. She did receive a claim payment.

Don't assume your situation will work out that well. If you are told you must answer questions under oath, be sure that a qualified public adjuster *and* a qualified attorney are on hand to offer you advice and representation.

Appendix B:
Voices From The
Front

IN 2007, I used an independent research firm to conduct a pilot survey of real-life policyholders who had filed a claim after experiencing damage, and *hadn't* worked with public adjusters in settling their claims. A fair number of the people surveyed, in my view, simply didn't understand or care about what they might have "left on the table" during negotiations – probably because they did not even know negotiating was an option.

Although some people were satisfied with the service and compensation their insurance company offered, many others sounded deeply disillusioned with the system. Here are some of the things policyholders said about their experiences with the claims process.

In their own words...

- "We had two or three inexperienced adjusters."
- "We didn't get all our costs reimbursed."
- "The problem was with the contractor not getting things done, and using shoddy materials. My problem was with an unethical contractor, who told

me he would take care of everything. He dealt directly with the insurance company."

- "We had a very high deductible. We didn't think we would have enough loss to file a claim, but when we started adding everything up, it was much more than we thought."
- "The estimator did not do a good job."
- "Some of the adjusters did not have the proper experience. Only part of the roof was covered, but they finally did cover it all after coming out more than three times."
- "There was a persistent lack of communication and misunderstanding by insurer of the actual damage. Insurer contracted out to an adjuster and they were only in loose communication. I had to intervene several times."
- "I got the runaround about paying for the house."
- "We just accepted it (the payment the insurance company offered). We didn't want to hire a lawyer."
- "Once we got past the faulty adjustor process, the insurance company paid quickly."
- "It (the claim settlement) should have been more."
- "They said it was water, not wind."
- "So many people were making claims, the insurance companies did not have to be in any hurry (to make a payment)."
- "It's a horrendous way to do business."

Appendix C:
Going It Alone?

OBVIOUSLY, in a book like this, it's impossible for me to teach you everything I've learned in the past twenty years of handling claims. So my first, and, I think, best advice to you would always have to be pretty simple: *consult a professional*.

Having said that, I realize that there are people who will refuse to hire someone else to do something they feel they can do by themselves. In this very short Appendix, my goal is give you enough information to help you improve your current, next, or even your previous claim – by an amount *many* times more than the cost of this book. (In my opinion, though, it is highly unlikely that you will do as well on your own as you would with a qualified public adjuster on your side.)

And yes, you read right. I said it is possible improve your *previous* claim. Believe it or not, you really can challenge a claim that the insurance company considers "closed." It all depends on things like how long ago the claim was, and under what circumstances it was settled or closed. I talk to people all the time who tell me they "never knew claims can be re-opened," or "never knew that claims can be renegotiated." It's in the insurance industry's financial interests, of course, for policyholders to believe that, once they cash a check, they can't come back to fix an error. It really is a shame how many people think this way. Mistakes happen, and your claim *can* be reopened and renegotiated. Here are some of the basics on how this happens.

Many insurance adjustment errors, especially on catastrophe claims, stem from the adjuster overlooking or mis-pricing damages. Usually, this happens for one of three reasons: adjusters don't spend enough time to identify all the damages; they are unfamiliar with the damaged item; or their estimating software incorporates a bad price.

Other mistakes happen when adjusters either misinterpret the policy or misinterpret the facts on the ground. Either circumstance can result in the denial of a claim that should actually be covered -- or in a payment that is lower than it should be.

If you decide to handle a claim yourself, or reopen one that you think deserves a second look, please consider yourself bound by the following ten "commandments" -- all of which a qualified public adjuster would scrupulously observe.

Commandment #1: Do not try to pull one over on your insurance company!

Be thorough, but be *honest*. Few things turn insurance adjusters on like the prospect of catching policyholders who are engaged in fraud. Most companies have entire departments devoted to rooting out fraud, and you can be sure that the insurance company's fraud representatives will be among the best-trained people in the company. (Too bad the adjuster who comes out to inspect your home probably isn't trained this well.). The fraud representatives have seen and heard it all, and they eat would-be cheats alive. Remember that insurance fraud is a crime. Don't even try it. And don't ask me to try it for you, because I won't!

And now: A side note. It seems a little unfair, doesn't it? The insurance company can make one "mistake" after another that costs you money, and you can be subjected to any number of mysterious coincidences that fall to the insurance company's benefit – coincidences that, taken together, can result in your claim being underpaid by thousands, tens of thousands, or even hundreds of thousands of dollars. And nothing bad ever seems to happen to the insurance companies (outside of record profits, I mean). But if an unscrupulous policyholder can be shown to be bumping his claim *up* by a few hundred bucks, that's *not* a coincidence. In that situation, you may rest assured that the insurance company *will* seek criminal charges if at all possible, even for what might seem by comparison to be fairly trivial amounts of money. What's more, it is very likely that the company will secure a conviction -- through the state, of course. A cynical person might wonder how even the playing field really is. I'll only point out that the insurance companies have the lobbyists, who, in turn, have the ear of lawmakers and other powerful folks.

Commandment #2: Take notes.

Buy a notebook. Buy a pen. Put them to use. Take your time and go around the property, noting everything you see to be damaged. Everything. Besides the obvious stuff like missing roofs and two-foot flood lines, you are looking for scratches, scuffs, scrapes, cracks, bangs, dents, tears, stains, discolorations, swelling, unevenness – I mean *everything*. Look high and low, inside and out. Write it all down.

You should also keep a detailed log of all conversations that take place with your insurance company, adjusters, contractors, and other players in this drama. Keep track of *everything:* Your own time cleaning up, time you spend making emergency and temporary repairs, and every penny you spend that has anything at all to do with the claim. I can't stress enough the importance of being thorough and detailed.

Commandment #3: Get pictures.

Photograph it all. Video it all. When I say "all," I mean *everything*. You may need these images somewhere down the line. Warning: Your adjuster may want a copy of these records. Be sure to keep copies for yourself in case the adjuster happens to lose the images you provide.

Commandment #4: Show the adjuster *all* the damage.

This sounds easy enough, but in order to do it, you must know exactly what to show them. Again, you're better off working with a professional who has done this a couple of hundred times. If you choose not to do that … well, be sure to give the adjuster a copy of your own exhaustive list of damage to the property, and keep a copy for yourself. Lead the adjuster around the property and be sure he or she notes each and every item on your list. If that means the visit takes two hours -- or ten hours -- so be it. *Be more thorough than the insurance company's adjuster wants to be.* I tend to find that if an adjuster is inspecting a property for 30 minutes, I will probably be there for two hours. If the adjuster is there for two hours, I will probably be there for four to six hours. Am I just slow on the uptake? I like to think not. I *am* thorough, though, and I *am* careful. I don't want to miss any damage. The adjuster wants to move on to the next claim. I want to make sure you get everything you're entitled to. Two different agendas!

Ask directly about the adjuster's experience level. You wouldn't want to be operated on by someone with little experience, and the same goes for the insurance adjustment of your largest financial asset, your home or business. Note that an ethical, experienced adjuster making any kind of effort should be able to point out a thing or two to you that wasn't on your list.

Commandment #5: Remind the adjuster that not all homes are built with the same materials.

Insurance adjusters use computerized estimating programs that are designed to generate *rough* estimates (or, as I prefer to call them, "guesses") about the *average* amounts of damage in *average* homes. These software programs tend to be fairly accurate in evaluating average homes and average losses – and tend to be less accurate on very small losses, very large losses, very low quality homes, or very high quality homes. The more familiar you are with your home and the quality of its construction, the better off you will be.

Commandment #6: Review the adjuster's completed estimate in detail, until you understand each and every line.

This is where you will find mistakes – unfortunately, though, these documents can be extremely tough to read. Room sizes may be off, damages you pointed out may have been omitted, or prices cited may be too low, either because the quality of the item being replaced is not correct, or because the prices being charged are higher than they were when the software for the estimating program was written. (This is a very common problem after a catastrophe).

Commandment #7: Have a licensed general contractor review the insurance company estimate and provide an independent estimate.

If this is impossible, at least see if they will indicate specific concerns they may have about the insurance estimate. This can be tough to do after a catastrophe, as contractors can be hard to come by. You may choose to get individual estimates from the roofer, carpenter, electrician, plumber, painter, A/C man, flooring specialist, or other professional. I would *not* suggest that you get estimates from the "cheapest guys in town." If you get more than one estimate for a particular repair, count on the insurance company paying on the *lowest* figure associated with whatever you provide them.

Commandment #8: If the insurance company refuses to pay for an item, demand that they explain (in writing) why.

The company should not only do this, but also show you exactly where in the policy it says that what you are claiming damages for is not covered. This point is very important. Never simply accept that something is not covered because the insurance company says it's not covered. The company has an obligation to make you understand *why* it is not covered. It is the company's job to *prove* to you that something is not covered.

Commandment #9: Be persistent. Don't give up.

This may be the most difficult commandment of all for you to follow, but it is absolutely essential. I am convinced that, as a group, U.S. policyholders walk away from millions of dollars in valid claims each year simply because they are sick and tired of dealing with the claims process. Hang in there. If it is appropriate to do so, write complaint letters to the company (making sure to cover the local, regional, and home office levels), as well as your state's regulatory agency, Attorney General, or Governor; your municipality's Mayor, Councilman, or Selectman; or anyone else in authority who may listen. Take advantage of any measures your policy or State has for reconciling these matters. (These are sometimes called *Alternative Dispute Resolution* methods.) When writing, be brief and to the point (I've seen people scribble page after page of ramblings that are impossible to make sense of. Even if they are right, these letters will never be taken seriously.) Keep after them. Be relentless. Try to stay calm.

Commandment #10: Seek professional assistance when needed.

Depending on the loss, this could mean a contractor, an engineer, a mold specialist, an accountant, an attorney – or, of course, you might decide that you need a good public adjuster after all. Again – *I will not charge you anything up front,* but will, instead, charge a commission on what I am able to collect for you above and beyond what the insurance company is offering. It may feel strange, having to consult with someone to make sure that your insurance company pays you what you're actually owed. But if they did what they were supposed to, I would be out of work.

I am your insurance against problems with the insurance company.

No, it's not "right" that you should need insurance like that, because you have probably been paying a large amount of money to the insurance company every month or quarter, and you've probably been doing that for years. But this is the way it is. At least now you know about it, and you also know what you can do about it.

Congratulations! Having made it this far, you are miles ahead of countless past victims of the insurance nightmare. May you stay that way. If you **ever** feel you're losing ground, **give me a call or write me**.

I truly hope you enjoyed my book, and that you learned from it as well.

If so, I would **greatly** appreciate it if you would take just a few minutes to write a review on the following sites:

www.Amazon.com
www.BN.com

Search for "Goldwich" and my book **UNCOVERED** should pop up.

It can be the same review, copied from one site to the other, and you don't have to use your real name (for insurance company employees worried what the boss may think). You can also email me your review.

I would like to personally hear about any questions, concerns or differences of opinion you have – just contact me.

Wishing You <u>More</u>!

Mark Goldwich

Mark Goldwich
1-800-523-2589
www.GoldStarAdjusters.com
Mark@GoldStarAdjusters.com

ABOUT THE AUTHOR

MARK GOLDWICH is a Florida native born and raised in Miami, and currently living in Jacksonville with his wife and two children.

In 1986, Mark earned a BSBA degree in Insurance from the University of Florida. He has been a licensed insurance adjuster in Florida since 1987, and is currently a licensed public adjuster in Florida and Georgia. He has also held licenses in Texas, Oklahoma, North Carolina, South Carolina, and Kentucky.

After seventeen years with one of the largest insurers of homes and autos in Florida and the nation, and after handling tens of thousands of claims from New York to California, and from Texas to Canada, Mark decided to put his decades of insurance experience to work for insurance victims. He has delivered settlements averaging 400% higher than the amounts initially proposed by insurance companies!

Mark is a licensed real estate professional, and a member of Windstorm Insurance Network, Inc., Jacksonville Regional Chamber of Commerce, and Mandarin Council's Small Business Leader of the Year for 2009.

Mark's mission is to educate insurance consumers everywhere, and to use his insurance expertise to represent his clients in effectively maximizing their settlements while minimizing their burden and frustration.

Contact him at:

Mark Goldwich
Gold Star Adjusters, LLC.
www.GoldStarAdjusters.com
Mark@GoldStarAdjusters.com
1-800-523-2589